ORESTES BROWNSON

Selected Political Essays

The Library of Conservative Thought

Orestes Brownson, *Selected Political Essays*, with a new introduction by Russell Kirk. 1990. ISBN: 0-88738-825-6

Victor A. Kravchenko, *I Chose Freedom*, with a new introduction by Rett R. Ludwikowski. 1988. ISBN: 0-88738-754-3

Victor A. Kravchenko, *I Chose Justice*, with a new introduction by Ludmilla Thorne. 1988. ISBN: 0-88738-756-X

William Hurrell Mallock, *A Critical Examination of Socialism*, with a new introduction by Russell Kirk. 1988. ISBN: 0-88738-264-9

Kenneth Shorey, ed., *John Randolph and John Brockenbrough: Their Correspondence*, with a new foreword by Russell Kirk. 1988. ISBN: 0-88738-194-4

George Scott-Moncrieff, *Burke Street*, with a new introduction by Russell Kirk. 1989. ISBN: 0-88738-250-9

John J. Stanlis, *Edmund Burke: The Enlightenment and Revolution*, with a new introduction by Russell Kirk. 1990. ISBN: 0-88738-359-9

Francis Graham Wilson, *The Case for Conservatism*, with a new introduction by Russell Kirk. 1990. ISBN: 0-88738-322-X.

ORESTES BROWNSON

Selected Political Essays

Edited by
Russell Kirk

With a new introduction by the editor

Transaction Publishers
New Brunswick (U.S.A.) and London (U.K.)

Originally published in 1955 by the Henry Regnery
Company as *Orestes Brownson: Selected Essays.*

Library of Congress Catalog Number: 89-28040
ISBN: 0-88738-825-6
Printed in the United States of America

Library of Congress Cataloging-in-Publication Data

Brownson, Orestes Augustus, 1803–1876.
    [Essays. Selections]
    Orestes Brownson Selected political essays / with a
new introduction by Russell Kirk.
        p.   cm.
    Reprint. Originally published: Selected essays. Chicago : Gateway Editions, 1955.
    ISBN 0-88738-825-6
    1. United States—Politics and government—1815–1861. 2. United States—Politics and government—1849–1877. 3. Equality—United States—History—19th century. 4. Representative government and representation—United States—History—19th century. 5. Church and state—United States—History—19th century. 6. Liberalism—United States—History—19th century. 7. Catholic Church—United States—History—19th century. I. Title.
E415.7.B78   1990   89-28040
322′.1′0973—dc20   CIP

CONTENTS

INTRODUCTION TO THE
TRANSACTION EDITION

Nothing is deader than dead politics, we have been told. Why, then, revive the political essays of the philosopher, polemicist, and Catholic publicist Orestes Brownson (1803–1897)?

We bring out this selection of Brownson's political writings because the questions raised by Brownson confront us still. The "American Idea," much discussed by Brownson, is especially relevant to our pressing concerns in 1989—both the fallacies about the "American Idea" that Brownson cudgeled, and certain truths about American society that Brownson discerned more clearly than did any other man in his time.

The American Republic, Brownson argued in his book by that title, is meant to reconcile liberty with law, and so set an example to the world. As he put it:

> Yet its mission is not so much the realization of liberty as the realization of the true idea of the state, which secures at once the authority of the public and the freedom of the individual— the sovereignty of the people without social despotism, and individual freedom without anarchy. In other words, its mission is to bring out in its life the dialectic union of authority and liberty, of the natural rights of man and those of society. The Greek and Roman republics asserted the state to the detriment of individual freedom; modern republics either do the same, or assert individual freedom to the detriment of the state. The American Republic has been instituted by Providence to realize the freedom of each with advantage to the other.[1]

In our present era of debate about global democracy and democratic capitalism, Brownson's writings take on renewed meaning. The first scholar to revive discussion of Brownson's thought and life was Arthur M. Schlesinger, Jr. While an undergraduate at Harvard, Schlesinger wrote his honors essay about Brownson's radicalism and heterodoxy early in his adult life; this study was published in 1939 as *Orestes A. Brownson: A Pilgrim's Progress.*

During the past half-century, in part because of the influence of Schlesinger's book, a good deal has been published about Brownson, at one time "a Marxist before Marx," but after 1844, a social conservative and a Catholic. Among the more recent studies are Leonard Gilhooley's *Contradiction and Dilemma: Orestes Brownson and the American Idea* (1972); Hugh Marshall's *Orestes Brownson and the American Republic* (1971); Per Sveino's *Orestes A. Brownson's Road to Catholicism* (1971); Gilhooley's symposium *No Divided Allegiance: Essays in Brownson's Thought* (1980); and *The Brownson Reader*, edited by Dr. Alvan S. Ryan (1955). In addition, there are other studies published earlier or later than the above, as well as a huge one-volume life by Father Thomas R. Ryan, *Orestes A. Brownson: A Definitive Biography* (1976). I have discussed Brownson's thought at some length in *The Conservative Mind* (1953) and in *The Roots of American Order* (1975).

Thus Brownson has re-entered America's political discourse. The line commonly attributed to President John F. Kennedy, "Ask not what your country can do for you, but what you can do for your country," was actually first uttered by Orestes Brownson at Dartmouth

College. "There are no lost causes," T. S. Eliot instructs us, "because there are no gained causes"—we fight the same battles in every century. Thus Brownson's redoubtable essays and speeches have become relevant to our discontents near the close of the twentieth century.

*   *   *

Born in Vermont while Thomas Jefferson was president, and dying in Detroit while Rutherford B. Hayes was president, Orestes Brownson knew practically everybody and wrote about practically everything in the nineteenth century. Brownson travelled from various forms of radicalism in politics and religion to political conservatism and religious orthodoxy. In his first principles he came to stand at the opposite pole from Ralph Waldo Emerson, whom he knew well. Among Brownson's friends was John C. Calhoun; it remains uncertain whether it was Calhoun or Brownson who first said that although it may be necessary for a man to sacrifice himself *for* the people, a man never should sacrifice himself *to* the people. It was Brownson who, a few months after publication of *The Communist Manifesto*, wrote a succinct reply to Marx (included in this volume of selections) that has not been excelled in prescience. Brownson set himself against both Abraham Lincoln and Jefferson Davis, arguing over and over again that authority and liberty both are necessary for a commonwealth.

All just authority is from God, Brownson kept reminding Americans. The fundamental error of Jacobins and Socialists is their illusion that merely human schemes can establish a terrestrial paradise. Like Tocqueville, Brownson declared that the American democracy is kept from tyranny by Christian moral habits. Indeed, Brownson was America's equivalent of John Henry Newman, with whom he corresponded and disputed.

Knowing poverty from his early years, Brownson was almost wholly self-educated. But what a schooling he gave himself! Lord Acton thought that Brownson possessed the most powerful mind of any American; and that was a high compliment, for it was the day of Hawthorne, Emerson, Melville, Calhoun, and other men of remarkable talents.

Brownson's course in political affairs and theological disputes is too intricate for close analysis here. Brownson found it necessary to grope his way through all the sects and factions of New England until he attained those concepts of divine and human nature after which his stubborn soul had yearned. He was a Bible reader from early childhood; his search for religious certitude led him from the Congregationalism of his early youth to Presbyterianism, Universalism, humanitarianism, Unitarianism, and Transcendentalism. He was a Universalist minister at one time, and at another a Unitarian preacher; he was active in the socialistic undertakings of Robert Owen and Fanny Wright; and for a year he was a militant atheist and a revolutionary conspirator.

But in none of these movements did he discover true reality. Somewhere, he concluded, there must exist a source of religious authority without which most men remain forever at sea; and he found this in the Catholic Church when he was forty-one years old. He was not always happy with the hierarchy of the church, nor the hierarchy with him; his relentless pen made him as many enemies among Catholics as among Protestants; and he encountered in America those difficulties which Newman confronted in Ireland—the brilliant convert debating with clerics who distrusted modernity and the presumption of the intellect.

His social ideas experienced mutations closely parrallel with those of his religious convictions. Long before the name of Marx was known, Brownson was a socialist; and in many respects he anticipated Marx's thought—which made him the more formidable as an adversary of socialism in his maturity. Besides, in his early years he was a complete democrat, taking equality for a natural right, and as the principle upon which the civil social existence ought to be ordered.

Brownson always believed that if a principle were sound, no danger would occur in pushing that principle to its logical consequences. This he did, in 1840, with his "Essay on the Laboring Classes," during the presidential campaign of that year. Equality of civil rights, he reasoned, should and must lead to equality of condition. The inheritance of private property, the system of bank credit, the modern industrial company, the factory system, and all the other principal features of what Marx would call "capitalism" must be abolished, it followed, so that equality of condition might triumph. Brownson advocated this thesis most stoutly; it did mischief to the cause of the Democratic party that he supported. Ironically enough, the election of 1840 disillusioned this unequivocal egalitarian. "We for one confess," Brownson wrote later, "that what we saw during the presidential election of 1840 shook, nay, gave to the winds all our remaining confidence in the popular democratic doctrines."[2]

After 1840, then, Brownson's drift toward conservative political convictions commenced. These convictions endured the rest of his life, and inclined him toward the moral authority of the Catholic Church. He had concluded from his close observation of the American people that pure democracy and economic equality were miserable shams, which could lead only to the destruction of freedom and justice and order. But if the principle of equality was false, upon what principle ought an intelligent citizen to found his politics? Brownson came to perceive that somewhere there must reside an authority, in the original Latin meaning of that word—a source of moral knowledge, a sanction for justice and order. Concluding that the expression of such an authority was the Catholic Church, he found that his search for social principle and his search for religious principle converged in 1844.

Brownson's political convictions were those of a religious man, not those of a Benthamite who looks upon the Church as a moral police force. Brownson understood that we cannot separate the realm of spirit and the realm of society into distinct entities; but he had no intention of using the Church to advance political causes, or of using his political activities to advance the interests of the Church. Religion and politics are joined in this: mundane justice and order require a moral sanction; and that sanction cannot be found outside religious principle. These were his mature views; and, knowing radicalism from the inside, Brownson was the better prepared for his onslaught upon pure democracy and socialism.

*   *   *

His style, like much of his life, reminds one somewhat of William Cobbett's. Like Cobbett, Brownson courted no man's favor; he was as vehement against the utilitarian philosopher and the money-obsessed entrepreneur as against the Marxist fanatic and the doctrinaire social revolutionary. Although a powerful polemicist, Brownson had not Cobbett's command of the language. I introduced T. S. Eliot to Brownson's writings in 1953, 1954, and 1955. In a holograph postscript to a letter Eliot wrote to me on January 13, 1956, he added, "I am not altogether pleased by Brownson's style, which strikes me as wordy and diffuse. But it is remarkable that a Yankee a century ago should have held such views as his, and depressing that he has been so ignored that most of us had never heard of them."

Eliot's strictures on Brownson's style notwithstanding, there are many memorable sentences and paragraphs in his political essays, the bulk of which is gigantic. His *Works*, in twenty ponderous double-column volumes, were published at Detroit between 1882 and 1887. In recent years, they have been made available in a very costly reprint edition. His book *The American Republic: Its Constitution, Tendencies, and Destiny* (1866) has been brought out by reprint houses as well. Brownson's other political volumes are extremely difficult to obtain—the most important of which is *Essays and Reviews, Chiefly on Theology, Politics, and Socialism* (1852).

The political argument of this indefatigable controversialist I endeavor to condense, below, into a few insufficient paragraphs. Brownson maintained that pure democracy and social equality are death to civilization and liberty; that the moral principles taught by the Church deny the rectitude of a leveling egalitarianism; and that men who would preserve the justice and the freedom of the American Republic must set their faces against the degradation of the democratic dogma.

Americans have misunderstood and misused the word *democracy,* Brownson writes. For democracy is simply a means of government and is not identical with liberty or justice or republicanism; but since the word is entrenched among us, we ought to try to apprehend it properly. Therefore, Brownson distinguishes between the old American territorial democracy founded upon local rights and common interests of the several states and smaller organs of society, and the pure democracy of Rousseau, which later writers call "totalitarian democracy."

Americans must endeavor with all the strength that is in them, Brownson thunders, to prevent the corruption of their old territorial institutions into a unitary state, intolerant of minorities and of all things established by prescription. This concept enters into all of Brownson's discussions of American politics. He entertained a high opinion of Calhoun's mind, but when the Civil War began, Brownson (who had detested Abolitionists and Fire-Eaters with impartial cordiality) remained a staunch Unionist, and at the end rejoiced in the Union victory (though he reproached Lincoln) as the triumph of genuine territorial democracy over the abstractions of Rousseau.

Socialism, Brownson tells us, is the application of the theory of pure democracy to economic life; and it must end in the ruin both of economic prosperity and of true social justice. He seems to have been the first writer of note to denounce Marxism as a heresy from Christianity—a concept recently affirmed by Christopher Dawson, Arnold Toynbee, Martin D'Arcy, and Reinhold Neibuhr. Brownson believes that true justice is the classical principle of "to every man the things that his nature requires"; he believed socialistic compulsory leveling is a perversion of the Christian doctrine of charity. Because he never falls into the opposite error of pure Benthamism, Brownson is the most convincing American adversary of Marxism.

Against liberalism, Brownson is no less forthright. His essay "Liberalism and Progress" is perhaps the best expression, in a few thousand words, of the American conservative stand. "The great misfortune of modern liberalism," he wrote, "is that it was misbegotten of impatience and born of a reaction against the tyranny and despotism of governments and the governing classes, and it is more disposed to hate than to love, and is abler to destroy than to build up."[3]

Brownson fought against several enemies of authority and justice. First, he had to contend against the radical doctrine of the Rights of Man—not the natural law of the Schoolmen, but the arrogant Rights of Paine and Priestley, quite severed from tradition. Second, he had to deal with the delusion of *vox populi vox Dei,* which presumptuous men, in America most of all, put forward as an excuse for majorities to alter all laws as they might choose, regardless of the rights of persons and minorities. Third, he was confronted by a belligerent individualism—in part a peculiarly American growth, in part the spirit of the age—which endeavored to subordinate all continuity and coherence and tradition to the immediate gratification of impulse. Fourth, he struggled against a Rousseauistic sentimentality that mistook a misty-eyed compassion for commutative justice. Fifth, he defended classical justice against an optimistic secularism which looked upon sin as a mere vestigial survival of barbarous times, certain to vanish with the march of progress. Sixth, he had to stand fast against the disintegrating competition of sectarianism, which, in denying the principle of authority and exalting private judgment, hewed at the foundation of justice: for justice is built upon authority, the authority of a general moral order of transcendent sanction.

Although Brownson often makes his case in these controversies with force and penetration, it is not as a wholly original thinker that he deserves to be read. What Brownson accomplished in his time was rather to apply such moral concepts to the raw new American society, telling Americans, how even they, in their triumphant materialism and swaggering individualism, could not long endure without true justice. In reminding Americans that they must respect the wisdom of their ancestors, he did not make himself popular with the innovating democracy. His work is difficult to trace in its subtle influence upon later generations; but it has done something to chasten and discipline American impulsiveness; and perhaps his admonitions have a greater meaning today than they did when Brownson died.

NOTES

1. Brownson, *The American Republic: Its Constitution, Tendencies and Destiny* (New York: P. O'Shea, new edition, 1866), p. 5.
2. Brownson, "Democracy and Liberty," *The Democratic Review* (April, 1843), in Brownson, H.F. (ed.), *The Works of Orestes Brownson* (Detroit: Nourse, 1892–1907), vol. XV, pp. 258–59.
3. Brownson, "Liberty and Progress," Brownson's Quarterly Review (October, 1864), in *Works of Orestes Brownson, op. cit.*, vol. XX, pp. 343–48.

CHAPTER ONE

THE PRESENT STATE OF SOCIETY*

NOTE ON "THE PRESENT STATE OF SOCIETY"

This essay, published in the *Democratic Review* for July, 1843, represents Brownson's convictions shortly after he had abjured all forms of radicalism, and as he stood just outside the Catholic Church. Brownson, reviewing Carlyle's *Past and Present* rises to a stern exhortation of his own, rejecting the fallacies of the socialistic reformers, but reminding the clergy and the masters of industry that their duties are ordained by God, and that the present distorted face of society reflects a gnawing sickness which they must try with all their power to remedy. He invokes the medieval past, not for simple imitation in our time, but for its example of faith and purpose. I do not know of anything published in the past several years quite so pertinent to our present discontents, more than a century after Brownson wrote this article.

*　　*　　*

[From the *Democratic Review* for July, 1843.]

Whatever the book he writes, Mr. Carlyle may well adopt from Schiller for his motto, *Ernst ist das Leben;* for although he plays many pranks, and cuts many literary capers, which are not much to his credit, life with him is a serious affair, and he writes always with an earnest spirit, for a high, noble, and praiseworthy end. He may often offend our fastidiousness, he may often vex or disappoint us by the vagueness or defectiveness of his views, but we can

---

* Past and Present. By Thos. Carlyle. Boston: 1843.

never read him without having our better feelings quickened, and getting a clearer insight into many things. We have come even to like his style,—that is, in him and for him, though by no means in and for others. It is natural, free from all literary primness and affectation, sincere, earnest, forcible,— admirably adapted to all the varieties and shades of thought, and moods of mind of the writer; responding with singular felicity to all the natural undulations of the soul; and, when read aloud, to those of the voice. This is especially true of the *History of the French Revolution*,—a great work, and almost the only one in our language deserving the name of history, and before which your Robertsons, Humes, Mackintoshes, and brotherhood, shrink to their proper dimensions.

Carlyle is a thorough master of language. We know no writer, ancient or modern, who so clearly apprehends the deep significance of speech; or so fully comprehends the profound philosophy there is in the ordinary terms of every-day life. True is it, in more senses than one, that our only sure way of arriving at psychology is through the medium of words; and not at psychology only, but at philosophy, the everlasting truth and fitness of things. All speech is significant; and if blest with clear insight we may seize the profoundest and most far-reaching truth, by turning over a very familiar word, and looking at it in the light of the primitive fact it was used to designate. One sees this in the half-serious, half-sportive remarks of Plato on the origin of names in the Cratylus, and specially in Vico's tract on the *Wisdom of the Ancient Italians, as collected from the Latin language.* There is scarcely a page, scarcely a sentence even, in Carlyle, in which he does not throw a new and surprising light on some intricate subject, by a dexterous use of a very familiar word. He lays open the word, and makes you see the fact, the thing, of which it was originally the sign, and of which it is still the sign, if the sign of aught. True, all this is done very quietly, by using a capital initial letter, italicising a syllable, separating a compound word into its original elements, or by giving a Latin equivalent for an Anglo-Saxon term, or an Anglo-Saxon one for a Latin; and since it is done so quietly, it is no doubt overlooked by the great majority of his readers, who, because they overlook it, call him obscure and unintelligible. "I do not understand you." "Sir, I am under no obligation to furnish you ideas and brains also." True, dear Doctor Johnson, but if we do not furnish our readers brains as well as ideas, how large a proportion of them will catch even a glimpse of our meaning on the most familiar topics we discuss? To perceive another's sense, or sense in another's words, we must have some little sense of our own;—a melancholy fact, and which will delay some weeks the complete success of our excellent societies for the Universal Diffusion of Knowledge.

There is no wisdom in sneering at him who truly studies words. Words, even the idlest, are signs, and signs of things, realities, which things, realities, are to be come at only through the signs. The term *God* and the adjective *good,* are one and the same word; and from this we learn that our Anglo-Saxon ancestors called by one and the same name, the supreme being, and that which it is proper to be, to desire, to do, or to possess. Therefore, say our wise modern philosophers, our Anglo-Saxon ancestors believed that the supreme being is good; thus proving that Balaam's ass, or rather that Balaam himself, yet liveth and speaketh. Say, rather, therefore, they believed and incorporated into their every-day speech, the great truth, the foundation and spring of all heroism, that nothing is proper to be sought after, to be done, or possessed, which is not Godlike, or divine. They found not God in good; but good in God. What shall I be? A *God*-man, God-like. What shall I do? That which is God-like. What shall I prize? A God-ly soul. They did not conceive of Good, independent of God,—make that conception the standard, and bring God to it, as before a tribunal, to ascertain whether he conformed to it, or not; but they regarded God himself as the standard, and whatever conformed to him, they called *good*, and said, That be, do, possess, live for, die for,—nothing else is worth a wish or a thought.

We note in Carlyle, with great pleasure, an unceasing effort to make his readers remark the significance, the wonderfulness of what is ordinary and familiar. To him the thaumaturgic WORD sounds out from all, from the least as well as from the greatest; and the Infinite is spoken by the grain of sand, as well as by Andes or Himaleh. Even silence is eloquent to him, and the dumb are not mute. He has a truly genial and loving soul,—a ready sympathy with and for all in God's universe. There is at times something startling and fearful in this universal sympathy, and the unexpected analogies it enables him to discover and disclose. All nature becomes sacred;

the universe a temple; each living thing, each thought, each feeling a shrine; we stand on holy ground; we fall down and worship; we are filled with awe; we hold our breath; we feel that we are in the very Sanctum, the very PRESENCE of the Infinite God.

But it is not our intention to enter into any inquiry concerning the general or particular merits, characteristics, or peculiarities of Mr. Carlyle. He is no stranger to the American public. This much, however, we may say, that he is almost the only contemporary English writer of much note, whose writings give us any signs of vitality, or that promise to leave any trace on his age or country. Your Wordsworths, Talfourds, Wilsons, Broughams, Macauleys, Bulwers, and the like—*Ernst ist das Leben,* we have no time to waste. Bulwer, we are told, has given up romancing, and betaken himself to serious study; we hope that he will yet do somewhat that will survive, by a few years, the natural term of his pilgrimage. Carlyle, with all his faults, is the only *live* Englishman it is our good fortune to know; and he, though alive, we are sorry to see, like all his countrymen, is *ailing.* Yet most thankful are we, that in these days of Cant and Humbug, Puseyism and Chartism, Communisms and Manchester Strikes, there is even one Englishman, who though ailing is not dead nor dying. God's blessing on him! May he soon be restored to perfect health, and it be long before he needs his Viaticum!

The book before us is a remarkable, but a melancholy production; it is the wail of a true manly heart, over the misery and wretchedness he sees everywhere around, and from which he himself is not exempt. No man sees more clearly the comic, or feels more keenly the tragic there is in our age, especially our English and American portion of it; yet no one views with a truer or more loving spirit the universal wrongs and sufferings of our Saxon race. He is sadly, nay, at times terribly in earnest; but his voice loses never its melody in becoming indignant; his heart is grieved, and his soul is sick, and his whole being laments over the miseries, the meannesses, the cants, the emptinesses, the quackeries, of the evil times on which we have fallen; but he laments in sorrow, not in wrath,—in anguish of spirit, but not altogether without hope. In his very severity, in his most scorching rebukes, he is mild, tolerant, loving to all that *is;* intolerant only to sham, mere make-believe, vacuity, Nothing pretending to be Something. We like his earnestness, and also the cheerfulness, so to speak, which he maintains even in his profoundest sorrow.

We cannot undertake to give any thing approaching an analysis of the very remarkable book before us, decidedly the best Carlyle has yet given us. It is unlike any thing else ever written by any other man, and no critical review can give the reader not acquainted with the general character of Mr. Carlyle's writings, the least conception of it. It has a purpose, or rather many purposes,—a general bearing, and many special and particular bearings; but these are not to be summed up and given in a line; they come out from the book as a whole, and can be gathered only by a close and attentive, we may say, a frequent reading of the whole book. The great aim of the writer is not to teach one lesson, but many lessons; and these not so much by formal statements, as by presenting the various topics on which he touches, in such light, or rather lights, as shall compel the reader to see and feel their significance, and draw his own moral.

Mr. Carlyle divides his work into four books; the first he entitles Proem; the second, The Ancient Monk; the third, The Modern Worker; the fourth, Horoscope. The work properly presents us, though in a strange, fitful, indirect, striking, not always satisfactory light, society as it was under feudalism and the Catholic church; society as it now is under the Protestant and industrial order; with some glances at what it should and must become if it is to be at all. What was yesterday? What is to-day? What do you propose for to-morrow? You are not where you were; you cannot remain where you are; whither are you tending? How will you arrive *there?* These are great questions, on which we shall do well to linger awhile.

The book opens with a chapter headed Midas, in which we have a sketch of the present state of life in England, not as tourists may represent it, but as it actually is. We extract the greater part:

"England is full of wealth, of multifarious produce, supply for human want in every kind; yet England is dying of inanition. With unabated bounty the land of England blooms and grows; waving with yellow harvests; thick-studded with workshops, industrial implements, with fifteen millions of workers, understood to be the strongest, the cunningest and the willingest our earth ever had; these men are here; the work they have done, the fruit they have realized is here, abundant, exuberant on every hand of us: and behold, some baneful fiat as of enchantment has gone forth, saying, 'Touch it not, ye workers, ye master-workers, ye master-idlers; none of you can touch it, no man of you shall be the better for it: this is enchanted fruit!' On the poor workers such fiat falls first, in its rudest shape; but on the rich master-workers too it falls; neither can the rich master-idlers, nor any richest or highest man escape, but all are like to be brought low with it, and made 'poor' enough, in the money-sense or a far fataller one.

"Of these successful skilful workers, some two millions, it is now counted, sit in Workhouses, Poor-law Prisons; or have 'out-door relief' flung over the wall to them—the workhouse Bastille being filled to bursting, and the strong Poor-law broken asunder by a stronger. They sit there, these many months now; their hope of deliverance as yet small. In workhouses, pleasantly so named, because work cannot be done in them. *Twelve hundred thousand* workers in England alone; their cunning right-hand lamed, lying idle in their sorrowful bosom; their hopes, outlooks, share of this fair world, shut in by narrow walls. They sit there, pent up, as in a kind of horrid enchantment; glad to be imprisoned and enchanted, that they may not perish starved. The picturesque Tourist, in a sunny autumn day, through this bounteous realm of England, descries the Union Workhouse on his path. 'Passing by the Work-

house of St. Ives in Huntingdonshire, on a bright
day last autumn,' says the picturesque tourist, 'I
saw sitting on wooden benches, in front of their
Bastille and within their ring-wall, and its railings,
some half hundred or more of these men. Tall,
robust figures, young mostly or of middle age; of
honest countenance, many of them thoughtful and
even intelligent looking men. They sat there, near
by one another; but in a kind of torpor, especially
in a silence, which was very striking. In silence:
for, alas, what word was to be said? An earth all
lying round, crying, Come and till me, come and
reap me;—yet we here sit enchanted! In the eyes
and brows of these men hung the gloomiest expression, not of anger, but of grief and shame and
manifold inarticulate distress and weariness; they
returned my glance with a glance that seemed to
say, "Do not look at us. We sit enchanted here,
we know not why. The sun shines and the earth
calls; and by the governing powers and impo-
tences of this England we are forbidden to obey.
It is impossible, they tell us!" There was something that reminded me of Dante's Hell in the
look of all this; and I rode swiftly away.'

"So many hundred thousands sit in workhouses,
and other hundred thousands have not yet got
even workhouses; and in thrifty Scotland itself,
in Glasgow or Edinburgh City, in their dark lanes,
hidden from all but the eye of God, and of rare
benevolence the minister of God, there are scenes
of woe and destitution and desolation, such as one
may hope the sun never saw before in the most
barbarous regions where men dwelt. . . . Descend

where you will into town or country, by what
avenue you will, the same sorrowful result dis-
closes itself; you have to admit that the working
body of this *rich* England Nation has sunk or is
fast sinking into a state to which, all sides of it
considered, there was literally never any parallel.
At Stockport assizes a mother and father are arraigned and found guilty of poisoning three of
their children, to defraud a 'burial society' of some
3 £. 8s. due on the death of each child; they are
arraigned, found guilty, and the official authorities,
it is whispered, hint that perhaps *the case is not
solitary, that perhaps you had better not probe
further into that department of things.* 'Brutal
savages, degraded Irish!' mutters the idle reader
of newspapers, barely lingering on this incident.
Yet is an incident worth lingering on; the depravity, savagery and degraded Irishism, being
never so well admitted. In the British land, a
human mother and father, of white skin, and
professing the Christian religion, had done this
thing; they, with their Irishism and necessity and
savagery, had been driven to do it. Such instances
are like the highest mountain apex emerged into
view, under which lies *a whole mountain region
and land, not yet emerged.* A human mother and
father had said to themselves, What shall we do
to escape starvation? We are deep sunk here,
in our dark cellar, and help is far. Yes, in the
Ugolino hunger-tower stern things happen; best-
loved little Gaddo fallen dead on his father's
knees! The Stockport mother and father think and
hint: Our poor little starveling Tom, who cries

all day for victuals, who will see only evil, and not good in this world; if he were out of misery at once; he well dead, and rest of us perhaps kept alive? It is thought and hinted, at last it is done. And now Tom being killed, and all spent and eaten, is it poor little starveling Jack that must go, or poor little starveling Will? What an inquiry of ways and means!"—pp. 1-4.

These individual instances show to those who will think, the abject misery and wretchedness to which the working population of England is reduced. What poverty! and this too in England, the richest nation on earth, perhaps the richest the world ever saw; and in England now, richer, with a greater abundance of supply for every want than at any former period! Think of this, linger long, oh, reader, and thoughtfully on this, for it is full of instruction.

"Nor are they," continues Mr. Carlyle, "of the St. Ives workhouses, of the Glasgow lanes, and Stockport cellars, the only unblessed among us. This successful industry of England, with its plethoric wealth, has as yet made nobody rich; it is an enchanted wealth, and belongs yet to nobody. We might ask, which of us has it enriched? We can spend thousands where we once spent hundreds, but can purchase nothing good with them. In poor and rich, instead of noble thrift and plenty, there is idle luxury alternating with mean scarcity and inability. We have sumptuous garnitures for our life, but have forgotten to *live* in the middle of them. It is an enchanted wealth; no man as yet can touch it. The class of men who feel that they are truly better off by means of it, let them give us their name!

"Many men eat finer cookery and drink dearer liquors—with what advantage, they can report, and their doctors can; but in the heart of them, if we go out of the dyspeptic stomach, what increase of blessedness is there? Are they better, beautifuller, stronger, braver? Are they even what they call happier? Do they look with satisfaction on more things and human faces, in this God's earth; do more things and human faces look with satisfaction on them? Not so. Human faces gloom discordantly, disloyally on one another. Things, if it be not mere cotton and iron things, are growing disobedient to man. The master worker is enchanted, for the present, like his workhouse workman; clamors, in vain hitherto, for a very simple sort of 'liberty': the liberty 'to buy where he finds it cheapest, to sell where he finds it dearest.' With guineas jingling in every pocket, he was no whit richer; but now, the very guineas threatening to vanish, he feels that he is poor indeed. Poor Master Worker! And the Master Unworker, is not he in a still fataller situation? Pausing amid his game-preserves with awful eye,—as he well may! Coercing fifty-pound tenants; coercing, bribing, cajoling; doing what he likes with his own. His mouth full of loud futilities, and arguments to prove the excellence of his corn-law; and in his heart the blackest misgivings, a desperate half-consciousness that his excellent corn-law is *inde*fensible, that his loud arguments for it are of a kind to strike men too literally *dumb*.

"To whom then is the wealth of England wealth? Who is it that it blesses; makes happier, wiser, beautifuller, in any way better? Who has got hold of it, to make it fetch and carry for him, like a true servant, not like a false mock-servant; to do him any real service whatsoever? As yet no one. We have more riches than any nation ever had before; we have less good of them than any nation ever had before. Our successful industry is hitherto unsuccessful; a strange success, if we stop here! In the midst of plethoric plenty, the people perish; with gold walls, and full barns, no man feels himself safe or satisfied. Workers, Master Workers, Unworkers, all men come to a pause; stand fixed, and cannot farther. Fatal paralysis spreading inwards, from the extremities; in St. Ives workhouses, in Stockport cellars, through all limbs, as if towards the heart itself. Have we actually got enchanted, then; accursed by some God?

"Midas longed for gold, and insulted the Olympians. He got gold, so that whatsoever he touched became gold, and he, with his long ears, was little the better for it. Midas had misjudged the *celestial music-tones;* Midas had insulted Apollo and the gods: the gods gave him his wish, and a pair of long ears, which also were a good appendage to it. What a truth in these old fables!"—p. 5-6.

"We have more riches than any nation ever had before, we have less good from them than any nation ever had before." England, with fifteen millions of workers, with machinery increasing man's productive power many thousand fold, making cotton at two-

pence an ell, and yet some five millions of her population sustained just above the starving point, and
not always *above* it! What a theme for reflection
here! Has the productive power of this God's rich
and glorious earth become exhausted? Is there not
yet room on its broad and inviting surface for many
millions more of workers; are there not yet immense
tracts waiting to be tilled; immense treasures yet to
be dug from the fertile soil? Whence comes then this
strange anomaly, that men with cunning brains, well-
made bodies, strong and active limbs, can find no
work to do, whereby even the simplest means of
subsistence may be obtained? Here lies the question.
The tendency is throughout all Christendom to bring
us to the point not only where no small portion of
the population can obtain the lowest wages for work
done, but where they can obtain no work to do. Already in England has it come to this. Millions say,
"Let us work,—for the love of God let us work, and
give us in return the humblest fare and the scantiest
clothing, so we do but keep the life in us, and we will
be forever grateful."

Vain prayer! "Ye naked, starving, begging workers, there is no work for you; ye have already worked
too much; ye have already produced more than we
can find markets for; ye are suffering from over-
production."

"Over-production. Just Heaven, what meaneth
this? We have made too many shirts to have a shirt
to our back; grown too much corn to be allowed to
have a loaf to keep the breath in the bodies of our

wives and little ones! *Over-production,* is it? Ha, ha, warehouses and corn-ricks can burn! Torches, torches there! We will soon put an end to this over-production."

So will, and may, and do, we had almost said, *should,* desperate men, forced to the starving point, reply to the taunt of over-production. These million workers, in the Manchester insurrection, last summer, striking work, standing mute, looking gloomily, are significant of much, and may tell Master Workers and Master Unworkers, that the mute will ere long find a tongue, and the dumb will speak, and through harsh brazen throats, startling them from their soft beds, to behold factory and palace sending up their red lights on the midnight sky; ay, and it may be, to behold royal and noble blood flowing once and again on the *Place de Grève.* Millions of hands striking work, because no work is to be had whereby men can keep the breath in them, will soon find work, and that of the direfullest sort. It is not we that say it, it is all history that says it, it is the human heart that says it. Master Workers and Master Unworkers, look to it, that ye press not the masses beyond the bearable point. Poor humanity will bear much, go for long ages with sorrowful eye and haggard face, bent to the earth; patient as the dull ox; but there is a point where, if submission does not cease to be a virtue, it at least ceases to be a possibility; and nothing remains but for her to draw herself up and turn upon the tyrant and battle it out. Better die struggling for freedom, for life, than to die timid, crouching slaves, to be buried in graves of our own digging.

We understand,—we believe nothing of this modern doctrine of the *legal* right of revolution; nor do we believe that violent revolutions are the best method of working out social reforms, and advancing humanity in freedom, religion, morality, well-being. In all countries where there is anything like established order, or where there is a governing body that admits but the slightest element of progress, and under which men *can* live; more especially in a country like ours, where there is a constitutional order in full force, which, if not perfect, yet contains in itself the elements of progress; we can countenance no measures of reform not allowed, not sanctioned by that order itself. But in this world there are specialties, and each of these specialties must always be decided on its own merits. In this country, as we have said over and over again for years, touching political organisms, we must be conservative, and study to preserve the order established by the wisdom of our fathers, aided by a beneficent and ever watchful Providence; because it is only by so doing that we can work out that higher order of civilization for mankind, which it is our mission to work out. But they know little of the spirit that burns in us, of the deep indignation we feel towards all who wrong or neglect their fellow men, and ride rough-shod over their brethren, who fancy that we hold or teach doctrines of tame, unqualified submission. While there is the least chink through which can reach us one, even the faintest, gleam of hope, we will submit and work on; but when the last gleam expires, when nothing remains but blackness and total extinction, we parley no more; we cease to discuss, to plead; we seize the brand and turn on the tyrant, and DIE shall he or we. It is an awful thing to see brother hewing and hacking the flesh of brother, and strewing the ground with the limbs and trunks of precious human beings; but it is more awful to see a whole nation of workingmen bound hand and foot, dying starved, while there is bread enough and to spare; a thousand times more awful in time of peace and plenty, to see poor human mothers driven to devour the flesh of their own offspring, of the dear ones who have drawn life from their own breasts!

But we must pass not too lightly over this subject. Can there be a more sorrowful sight, can there be a stronger condemnation of an order of things, than this simple fact of men, able-bodied men, with rational souls and cunning right hands, willing, begging to work, and yet finding no work to do whereby they can get their victuals? Certainly not, say all men with one voice. Well, then, friends and countrymen, is it only in England that we stumble on this fact? What, we ask, are we coming to in this country, here where there are so many millions of acres of rich, fertile lands, waiting to be tilled? We have not yet come, it may be, to the Glasgow lanes and Stockport cellars, of which Carlyle speaks, but we *have* come very near to the St. Ives workhouses; but we have come to the point where there are many thousands of our people who can keep the life in them only as fed by the grudging hand of public or private charity. In 1829, it was reckoned that in Boston, New York, Philadelphia and Baltimore, there were eighteen thousand females, sempstresses mostly, unable to obtain work for more than two-thirds of the time; and yet if getting work all the time, for sixteen hours a day, receiving therefor only about sixteen dollars a year with which to furnish fuel, food and clothing; many of these wives with sick and disabled husbands; many of them widows with two, three and four small children to support. So said the benevolent Matthew Carey. The matter must be worse now. In this wealthy, charitable, industrious, Christian city of Boston, where we now write, we have come, the last winter, to our bread and soup societies! Bread and soup societies for the poor, already in this blessed land of America, free, democratic America, and in the very heart of thrifty, religious New England! So alas! have we managed it. We may wince at the statement; may offer all manner of explanations of it, such as influx of foreigners, stagnation of trade, want of confidence, John Tyler administrations; but there stands the fact, in open, broad daylight, that able-bodied men and women, ready and willing to work for their food, nay, coming to you, and with tears in their eyes, begging you to give them work, have been kept through the long winter just above the starving point,—and we fear in all cases not above,—only by soup and bread dealt out by charitable societies in tin porringers. Just before the breaking out of the French revolution, some poor peasants came to the court, and asked for bread and got—a new gallows; which shows how it fares with the people under the monarchical method of governing. St. Ives work-houses, Glasgow lanes, Stockport cellars, and the present condition of Ireland, where, out of a population of eight millions, one-third are reduced to feed on third-rate potatoes, these scantily obtained, and failing altogether for nearly a third of the year, show how they manage matters under an aristocracy. Soup and bread societies for men and women able and willing to work, in Boston and other cities, show to what a pass things may come under the virtuous and intelligent rule of the democracy; which, considering the advantages with which we started, the vast quantities of fertile lands still lying waste, and our youth, vigor, and elasticity, is pretty well, and may be thought to prove that, if we have not as yet come up with kings and nobilities, we are in a fair way of overtaking them, and, if it were possible, of even going beyond them.

Here we are, then, in our own country, in the most favored part of it, renowned the world over for its industry, and thrift, frugality and economy, and wise management, come to such a pass that a portion —we will hope as yet not a large portion—of our population can get no work, no opportunity whereby to eat their bread in the sweat of their face. The fact is undeniable. It cannot be glossed over. It is here. We can lay our hands on it. These soup and bread societies are no fiction. Alas! the necessity there was that they should be, is also no fiction. With our own eyes we have seen poor children gliding along the cold streets, thinly clad, with their tin cans to receive their modicum. We have set our own feet in the miserable dwellings of those who have been thus fed, and knelt down in prayer by the poor man dying of a fever brought on by anxiety and insufficient food.

The newspapers told us some time since of a well educated, respectable man, brought up before our police for stealing a parcel from a dry goods shop.

On the trial, it came out that he was well nigh starved, could get no work, and had taken the desperate resolution of stealing in order to gain the *privilege* of being sent to the *House of Correction* so as not to die starved. To such straits had it come with him, that he regarded it as a favor to be sent to the House of Correction. A poor man, a worthy mechanic, in Philadelphia, this last winter, can find no work; comes to the magistrate and begs to be locked up in the cell of the City Prison; so that he may find the food which he knows no other method of procuring. One rejoices to know that the benevolent magistrate granted him his request.

Now, in all soberness, we ask, if a state of things in which such incidents can occur, do occur, however rare, is the best that we can have in this nineteenth century, in this blessed land of America, of universal suffrage, universal education, under the blessed light of the Gospel, dotted all over with industrial establishments, school-houses, and churches? Is this a God's world, or is it a devil's world? O, dear countrymen, say what you will, decidedly this is not a question for England only; it is also a question for you. In God's name, in humanity's name, do not blink this question. Answer us, nay, not us, but your own hearts, if you are prepared, in the face of that sun which shines so gloriously on all, the lowly thatched cottage as well as on the lordly palace, to say that you solemnly believe that in the decrees of Providence, in the richest of infinite Love, and of infinite Grace, there was nothing better for us than these bread and soup societies, this begging to be locked up in jail, and stealing in order to be sent to the House of Correction, so that the life may be left in us?

We might go further, in proof of the sad state to which we are coming or have already come. We are told, on tolerable authority, that in this city of Boston, which we take it is the model city of this country, there are some four thousand wretched prostitutes out of a population of about one hundred thousand. This fact is not only a lucid commentary on our morals, but also on the difficulty there is in getting a living by honest industry; since prostitution is resorted to in this and all other countries rarely through licentiousness, but chiefly, almost wholly, through poverty. We are also told by the agents of the police, who have the best means of knowing, that the principal supply of these victims to poverty and men's infamy, comes from the factories in the neighboring towns!—no uninteresting comment on the workings of the factory system, built up by our banks and high tariffs, and which the chiefs of our industry have taken, and are taking so much pains to fasten on the country!

But whence come these sad results? There must be somewhere a fatal vice in our social and industrial arrangements, or there would not, could not, be these evils to complain of. Never, till within these last few centuries, were men, able and willing to work, brought to the starving point in times of peace, and in the midst of plenty. "Gurth," says Carlyle, "born thrall of Cedric the Saxon, tended pigs in the wood, and did get some parings of the pork. The four-footed worker has already *got* all that the two-handed one is clamoring for. There is not a horse in all England, able and willing to work, but *has* due food and lodging; and goes about sleek-coated, satisfied in heart. Is this such a platitude of a world, that all working horses shall be well fed, and innumerable working men and women die starved?" We do not believe it; we will, thank Heaven! believe no such thing. Whence, where, and what, then, is the fundamental vice of our modern society, especially in this our Saxon portion of it?

On this question Mr. Carlyle's book throws some light, though, it must be owned, often of the fitful and uncertain sort. In general, and in rather vague terms, it may be answered that this vice is in the fact that men have substituted the worship of Mammon for the worship of God. Mammonism has become the religion of Saxondom, and God is not in all our thoughts. We have lost our faith in the noble, the beautiful, the just; we have lost our faith in the Highest, and have come to believe in and to worship the lowest, even Mammon,—

"Mammon, the least erected spirit that fell
From heaven; for even in heaven his looks and
    thoughts
Were always downward bent, admiring more
The riches of heaven's pavement, trodden gold,
Than aught divine or holy else enjoy'd
In beatific vision."

The demonstration of this fact, and a full and impartial description of the worship of Mammon, would be a service of no mean worth to our countrymen; but who shall undertake to perform it? The other day we chanced to drop a word which was misconstrued into a growing distrust of liberty, and voices in all parts of the country were loud and harsh in condemnation; should we now but *exercise* the liberty of telling our countrymen the simple truth, and of directing their attention to the error, the original sin whence has sprung the present disordered state of society, there would be no end to the berating we should receive from these same loud and harsh voices,—ready always to cry lustily for liberty, but most ready to condemn all who are really her efficient friends and servants. We boast, in this blessed land of Washington and Jefferson, of our freedom; we are free, ay, free as the winds that drive through our valleys or sweep over our broad plains and inland oceans,—to echo the public voice, to have no opinion of our own, and to say only what everybody believes or nobody takes the trouble to disbelieve. We knew, once upon a time, a young man, brought up in the wild freedom lingering yet in some few of our mountain homes; an earnest, simple spirit, who had the strange fancy when he came to dwell in cities and in the midst of civilization, that he should be sincere, transparent, and speak out always, when speaking at all, the simple, naked truth, without any circumlocution or reticence, as he found himself commanded by the Highest, and as all public Teachers and Able Editors exhorted him and all men to do. Foolish youth from the mountains! It was never intended by these Lights of their age, that thou shouldst *exercise* freedom of thought and freedom of speech, but merely that thou shouldst, in high-sounding and well-turned periods, laud freedom of thought and freedom of speech, and tell thy admiring countrymen what fine things, beautiful things they are. Poor young man! We own that, with all thy folly, we loved thee. Thou hadst a noble heart, a brave spirit, and we confess that we have watered with our tears the turf on thy early grave. But notwithstanding our inward admiration of thy free and generous nature, we have finally resolved to take warning by thy melancholy fate, and to be like our countrymen generally,—wise and prudent. Humbly do we beg pardon for having said in our folly, that what the demagogues tell them about their intelligence and virtue is all a humbug. It was an unwise, an imprudent word. We will no more repeat it. We will henceforth be silent, merely pointing, in our good city of Boston, to soup and bread societies for able-bodied men and women, ready, willing, begging to work, who yet can get no work to do; to four thousand victims of man's infamy, the number kept good by a surplus factory population; to the honest, intelligent, even well-educated man, driven to steal, in order to gain the, to him, inestimable favor of being sent to the House of Correction. Dear friends, most wise and virtuous demagogues, all you say of the dear people, of their intelligence and virtue, is, no doubt, very true, very sweet—for you have sweet breaths—and may we never be again left to question your veracity; but these four thousand . . . , these soup and bread societies, this privilege of being sent to the House of Correction, or of being locked up in a dungeon?

We have some thoughts on the origin of the evils we have touched upon, but which, were we to tell them all plainly, and honestly, and unreservedly, would, we fear, create such a hubbub and general confusion, that we should lose henceforth the power not only to be heard, but even to speak at all. There can be no question that within the last three hundred years there has been a most wonderful increase of industrial activity; of man's productive power; and of the aggregate wealth of the world. Great industries, so to speak, have within these three hundred years sprung up, never before conceived of; man has literally made the winds his messengers, and flames of fire his ministers; all nature works for him; the mountains sink, and the valleys rise before him; the land and the ocean fling out their treasures to him; and time and space are annihilated by his science and skill. All this is unquestionable. On the other hand, equally unquestionable is it to him who has looked on the matter with clear vision, that in no three hundred years known to us, since men began to be born and to die on this planet, upon the whole, it has fared worse, for soul or for body, with the great mass of the laboring population. Our advance, it would seem, has been that ordered by the militia captain, an "advance backwards!" This statement may or may not make sad work with our theories of progress of the race, progress of light, of political and social well-being, and all that: but it is a fact, an undeniable, a most mournful fact, which get over we cannot, try we never so hard.

For these last three hundred years we have lost or been losing our faith in God, in heaven, in love, in justice, in eternity, and been acquiring faith only in human philosophies, in mere theories concerning supply and demand, wealth of nations, self-support-ing, labor-saving governments; needing no virtue, wisdom, love, sacrifice, or heroism on the part of their managers; working out for us a new Eden, converting all the earth into an Eldorado land, and enabling us all to live in Eden Regained. We have left behind us the living faith of the earlier ages; we have abandoned our old notions of heaven and hell; and have come, as Carlyle well has it, to place our heaven in success in money matters, and to find the infinite terror which men call hell, only in not succeeding in making money. We have thus come— where we are. Here is a fact worth meditating.

We boast of our light; we denounce old feudalism and the middle ages, and fancy it worth a *Te Deum* that we have got rid of them; and yet, the impartial and clear-sighted historian being asked, what period he lingers on, when, all things considered, it proved best with the great mass of the European population, answers, without hesitation, the period when feudalism and the church were in their greatest glory; that is, from the tenth to the end of the fourteenth century. Compare the condition of what Carlyle calls the "workers" of England, the land of our ancestors, during that period, with the condition of the corresponding class at present, and one is almost struck dumb by the contrast. Cotton, as Carlyle says, is cheaper, but it is harder to get a shirt to one's back. Cotton is produced at two pence an ell, and shirts lie piled up in warehouses, and men go about with bare backs. For food, even Gurth born thrall of Cedric, did get some parings of the pork; the poor mother and father of the Stockport cellar, alas! none. For spiritual food, the poorest had faith and were instructed at least in the elements of the Christian religion; inquiries recently made into the condition of the population employed in the English collieries, show that human beings do grow up in the nineteenth century, in rich, ay, and *Christian* England, who know not even the name of their Maker, save by hearing it desecrated; and all accounts agree that the morals of the colliers are superior to the morals of the factory operatives. In the highest departments of thought and genius, the contrast is hardly less striking; our most advanced philosophers were anticipated; we are scarcely able even to copy the Gothic church, the last word of Christian architecture; and Dante has in poetry no rival, unless it be Shakspeare.

During these and the preceding four hundred years, more work was done for humanity, under an intellectual and social point of view, than was ever done, in a like period, since history began. A writer, not to be suspected of undue partiality, in touching upon this period and upon the action of the church, is forced to say, "During the greater part of that period, by means of her superior intelligence and virtue, she—the church—ruled the state, modified its actions, and compelled its administrators to consult the rights of man, by protecting the poor, the feeble, and the defenceless. It is not easy to estimate the astonishing progress she effected for civilization during that long period called by narrow-minded and bigoted Protestant historians, the dark ages. Never before had such labors been performed for humanity. Never before had there been such an immense body, as the Christian clergy, animated by a common spirit, and directed by a common will and intelligence to the culture of the moral virtues and the arts of peace. Then was tamed the wild barbarian, and the savage heart made to yield to the humanizing influences of tenderness, gentleness, meekness, humility, and love; then imperial crown and royal sceptre paled before the crosier; and the representative of him who lived, and toiled, and preached, and suffered, and died in obscurity, in poverty and disgrace, was exalted and made himself felt in the palace and in the cottage, in the court and in the camp, striking terror into the rich and noble, and pouring the oil and wine of consolation into the bruised heart of the poor and friendless. Wrong, wrong have they been, who have complained that kings and emperors were subjected to the spiritual head of Christendom. It was well for man that there was a power above the brutal tyrants called emperors, kings, and barons, who rode rough-shod over the humble peasant and artisan,—well that there was a power, even on earth, that could touch their cold and atheistic hearts, and make them tremble as the veriest slave. The heart of humanity leaps with joy, when a murderous Henry is scourged at the tomb of Thomas à Becket, or when another Henry waits barefoot, shivering with cold and hunger, for days, at the door of the Vatican, or when a Pope grinds his foot into the neck of a prostrate Frederick Barbarossa. Aristocratic Protestantism, which has never dared enforce its discipline on royalty and nobility, may weep over the exercise of such power, but it is to the existence and exercise of that power that the *People* owe *their* existence, and the doctrine of man's equality with man, its progress."*

The writer here quoted, is hardly just to the feudal aristocracy. The old feudal lords and barons were not a mere dilettante aristocracy, a mere unworking aristocracy, consuming without doing aught for the general work of production. They were, in fact, then a working aristocracy, and did work in their rude way, and contrived to do no little work of the governing sort; for which the governed did fare the better. In matters of fighting they did the hardest, and bore the first and heaviest blows. It was their special right, not to lead only, but to do the work of killing and of being killed. They did in some sense, in return for what they received, yield a protection to the people, and take some kind of care of them. If the serf, before serfage was abolished, labored for his lord, the lord owed him a reciprocal obligation, and must see that he had wherewithal to eat and to be clothed. If fixed to the soil, the serf had a right to his support from it. These old barons, moreover, did not entirely neglect the commons in contending for the interest of their own order, as we may learn by consulting Magna Charta. The service they rendered to society, was no doubt an inadequate return for what they received; but nevertheless it was some return, and the castle of the Lord, *law-ward,* according to Carlyle, was a tower of strength not only to its owner, but also to the hamlet lying under its walls; and the proud dame, my Lady, *Loaf-distributor,* was not seldom a gentle benefactress to the humble, confiding, and grateful peasants. If it was a privilege to

* Ante. p. 67.

be high-born, so was it a privilege to have the high-born among us.

On this part of the subject, Mr. Carlyle's book may be consulted with considerable advantage. He has not said all he might, nor all that we wish he had. He has given us a very pleasant glimpse of one aspect of life in the middle ages, that represented by the Ancient Monk; but we wish it had comported with his plan to have given us a clearer insight into the condition of the rural population, the cultivators of the soil, the thralls, sockmen, farmers, peasants, and their relation to their landlords, masters, or owners. We confess that on this subject we are not so well informed as we would be. It is a great and interesting subject, but from the glimpses we catch now and then of it, we are fully convinced that the relation between the two classes which then subsisted, was decidedly preferable to that which now is; even your modern slaveholder is obliged to recognize a relation between him and his slave of a more generous and touching nature than any recognized by the master-worker between himself and his workman. The slave when old or sick must be protected, provided for, whether the owner receives any profit from him or not; the master-worker has discharged all the obligation to his operative he acknowledges when he has paid him the stipulated wages. These wages may be insufficient for mere human subsistence, and the poor worker must die; but what is that to the master-worker? Has he not paid all he agreed to pay, even to the last farthing, promptly? We have not heard on our southern plantations, of Stockport cellars, of bread and soup societies by the charitable, and men stealing in order to be sent to the House of Correction so as not to starve. This much we can say of the slave, that if he will tend pigs in the wood, he shall have some parings of the pork, and so long as his master has full barns he is not likely to starve; would we could say as much of the hired laborer always!

But the chief thing we admire in the middle ages, is that men did then believe in God, they did believe in some kind of justice, and admit that man, in order to reap, must in some way aid the sowing; that man did, whatever his condition, owe some kind of duty to his fellow man; and admit it, not merely in theory, in caucus speeches, or in loud windy professions, but seriously in his heart and his practice. But we have changed all that, we have called the religion of the middle ages superstition, the philosophy which then was cultivated, miserable jargon, and the governing which then went on, tyranny and oppression. We have learned to blush at the page of history which speaks of Hildebrand, and St. Anselm, and the enfranchisement of the communes, and would if we could blot it out. It is a reproach to a man in these times and in this country to name it without execrating it. The age which covered Europe over with its Gothic churches, and with foundations and hospitals for the poor, produced St. Anselm, Abelard, St. Bernard, and Dante, Chaucer, old John of Gaunt, and Magna Charta, De Montfort, William Longbeard, Philip Van Arteveld, Roger Bacon, Albert Magnus, John of Fidanza, Duns Scotus, and St. Thomas Aquinas, is a blank in human history! Thank God we have outgrown it, got rid of it. We are no longer

superstitious; we have made away with the old
monks whose maxim was "work is worship;" we
have struck down the last of the barons; we are free;
we have the Gospel of the cotton mill, *laissez-faire,*
save who can, and the devil take the hindmost, and
we can do what we please with our own. A notable
change this, and worth considering. How was it
brought about, and what has been the gain?

We cannot go fully into the inquiry this question
opens up. The middle ages brought the human race
forward not a little. What most strikes us is the
moral and spiritual exaltation which everywhere
meets us. Man, through the faith nurtured and
strengthened in him by the church, became great,
noble, chivalrous, energetic. This immense spiritual
force accumulated in the interior of man during the
four centuries named, overflows in the activity, bold
adventure, vast enterprises, and important discoveries which commence in the fifteenth century. We
note here four things resulting from it, which have
especially contributed to the change of which we
speak: the invention or rather general use of gunpowder; the revival of letters; the invention of printing; and the maritime discoveries in the East and the
West. These are considered, we believe, the principal
agents in effecting what we have been pleased to call
the progress of modern society.

1. The art of war, as carried on prior to the introduction of fire-arms, which did not come into general
use before the fifteenth century, was accessible for
the most part only to the noble class and their retainers. It required so long a training, so great bodily
strength and dexterity, and so much outlay in the

equipments of the individual warrior, that artisans and peasants could make up but a small part, and never a very efficient part of an army. The chief reliance was, and necessarily, upon the nobility, the knights, and gentlemen. In this case the king was always more or less dependent on his nobles, and could rarely go to war without their assent and active aid. This restrained the royal power, and prevented the *centralization* of power in the hands of the monarch. The invention and general use of fire-arms lessened the importance of the cavalry, in which only the lords and gentlemen served, and increased that of the infantry, composed of commoners. The monarch was able to dispense then, to a certain extent, with the services of his nobility, and to find his support in the people, artisans and peasants, easily collected and speedily disciplined. By thus introducing the infantry into the royal armies, as the main reliable branch of the service, a rude shock was given to the power and independence of the nobles. From that moment the feudal nobility began to wane, and the power and independence of the monarch to increase.

The decrease of the power of the nobility served to weaken that of the church. The people naturally, with their instinctive wisdom, would cleave to the monarch, who employed them in his armies. They saw themselves now admitted to a share in an employment which had been previously, for the most part, the prerogative of their masters, and proud of being admitted to the high privilege of killing and being killed, they fancied that they were by this admission virtually enfranchised, and raised to an equality with those who had hitherto been their superiors. The rudest peasant, with a firelock in this hand, was more than a match for the bravest, strongest, best diciplined, and completely armed knight. Hence, all the tendencies of the people would be, in any contest, so far as possible, to support their royal masters. In the commons, then, royalty found its support against the nobility, and even against the church. At least, by admitting the common people into the royal armies, royalty weakened, or to some extent neutralized their affection for the ecclesiastical power, which in any contest between it and the church was of vast importance.

2. The revival of letters, as it is called, that is, of the study and reverence of *heathen* literature, which followed the taking of Constantinople by the Turks, had also a powerful influence in bringing about the change we have noted. The church, during the middle ages, had paid great attention to education; it had covered Europe over with universities and schools. In the early part of the fifteenth century, education was almost as general throughout the principal states of Europe as it is now; the actual amount of instruction one is tempted to believe was greater, though perhaps a smaller number could read and write. The Bible had been translated into the vernacular language of Englishmen prior even to Wyckliffe, which would indicate that the Saxon population were able to read. There was, at any rate, a very general mental activity throughout Europe, as the relics of the popular ballads and literature of the time bear witness. The mind was prepared for the new literature which was then brought to light. The

Greek scholars, with Greek subtlety and Greek sophistry, were dispersed, by the taking of Constantinople, over the principal Latin States; the study of the ancient heathen literature went with them, and the several schools of ancient Greek philosophy had their disciples and champions in the very bosom and among the high dignitaries of the church herself. Its obvious and unquestionable superiority, as to the perfection and beauty of its form, over the richer, profounder, more varied, and earnest, but less polished literature of the fathers and the church, secured it a ready adoption and an almost universal authority. In this fact we are to discover a powerful cause operating to destroy the power of the church and the order of civilization it had built up.

During the preceding centuries the nobles, being almost wholly occupied with governing, fighting, and doing their part, as they could, in the general affairs of society, had left literature almost entirely to the church. But, in the fifteenth century, in consequence of the change already noted in the art of war, their original occupation was to a considerable extent taken away, and they began to turn their attention towards letters. The schools and universities began to send out scholars from the lay commoners, and we had for the first time in Europe, since the establishment of the barbarians, an educated and literary laity. The surface of education had been greatly extended; and alway in proportion as education extends laterally does it lose in depth. The diffusion of education among the laity had created an immense class of superficial thinkers, half-educated, always worse, more to be dreaded than those who have no education, as simplicity is always preferable to ignorance fancying itself wisdom. We had then just the state of mind necessary to welcome the heathen literature of which we speak. Its very superficialness, want of earnestness and strength, when compared with Christian literature, was recommendation, and facilitated its reception.

The effect of this revived heathen literature, on the tone of thought, and its general bearings on Christian faith, are not always duly considered. The fathers of the church in the first five centuries had culled out from it all that Christianity would assimilate to itself, and made it an integral part of the common literary and philosophic life of the church. We had in the church all of heathen Greece and Rome that was worth retaining, or that could be retained in consistency with our faith as Christians. The human race then did not need the revival. No good could come of it; for nothing new, but exploded heathenism, was to be obtained from it. The revival was then in very deed a revival of heathenism. It was hostile to Christianity, and deeply prejudicial to the faith of Christians. And so history has proved it. We speak advisedly. We know very well the estimation in which the ancient classics are held, and that one may as well speak against the Bible as against them. But, what is this so much boasted classical literature? We admit the exquisiteness of its form; the perfection of the execution; we, too, have our admiration for the divine Plato; we love as well as others an Aristotle, and find much in the Greek tragedians that we love and admire; but we cannot forget that the whole body of ancient Greek and

Roman literature is heathenish, wanting in true religious conception, in genuine love of man, in true, deep, living, Christian piety. Permit us to quote here, what we wrote on this subject some seven years ago, from another point of view, it is true, and with a far different aim, but still with substantially the same faith:

"By means of the classics, the scholars of the fifteenth century were introduced to a world altogether unlike, and much *superior* [perhaps not] to that in which they lived,—to an order of ideas wholly diverse from those avowed or tolerated by the church. They were enchanted. They had found the ideal of their dreams. They became disgusted with the present, they repelled the civilization effected by the church, looked with contempt on its fathers, saints, martyrs, schoolmen, troubadours, knights, and ministrels, and sighed and yearned, and labored to reproduce Athens or Rome.

"And what was that Athens and that Rome which seemed to them to realize the very ideal of the perfect? We know very well today what they were. They were material; through the whole period of their historical existence, it is well known that the material or temporal order predominated over the spiritual. * * * Human interests, the interests of mankind in time and space predominate. Man is the most conspicuous figure in the group. He is everywhere, and his imprint is upon everything. Industry flourishes; commerce is encouraged; the state is constituted and tends to democracy; citizens assemble to discuss their common interests; the orator harangues them; the aspirant courts them; the warrior and the statesman render them an account of their doings, and await their award. The *People*—not the gods—will, decree, make, unmake, or modify the laws. Divinity does not become incarnate, as in the Asiatic world; but men are deified. History is not theogony, but a record of human events and transactions. Poetry sings heroes, the great and renowned of earth, or chants at the festal board and at the couch of voluptuousness. Art models its creations after human forms, for human pleasure, or human convenience.

"There are gods and temples, and priests and oracles, and augurs and auguries, but they are not like those we meet where spiritualism reigns. The gods are all anthropomorphous. Their forms are the perfection of the human. The allegorical beasts, the strange beasts, compounded of parts of many known and unknown beasts, which meet us in Indian, Egyptian, and Persian mythology, as symbols of the gods, are extinct. Priests are not a caste, as under spiritualism, springing from the head of Brahma, and claiming superior sanctity and power as their birthright; but simple police officers. Religion is merely a function of the state. * * * Numa introduces or organizes polytheism at Rome, for the purpose of governing the people by means of appeals to their sentiment of the holy; and the Roman pontifex maximus was never more than a master of police.

"In classical antiquity religion is a function of the state. It is the same under Protestantism.

Henry VIII, of England, declares himself supreme head of the church, not by virtue of his spiritual character, but by virtue of his character as a temporal prince. The Protestant princes of Germany are *protectors* of the church; and all over Europe there is an implied contract between the state and the ecclesiastical authorities. The state pledges itself to support the church, on condition that the church support the state. Ask the kings, nobility, or even church dignitaries, why they support religion, and they will answer with one voice, 'Because the people cannot be kept in order, cannot be made to submit to their rulers, and because civil society cannot exist, without it.' The same, or a similar answer will be returned by almost every political man in this country: and truly may it be said, that religion is valued by the Protestant world as an auxiliary to the state, as a mere matter of police.

"Under the reign of spiritualism all questions are decided by authority. The church commanded, and men were to obey, or be counted rebels against God. Materialism, by raising up man and the state, makes the reason of man, or the reason of the state paramount to the commands of the church. Under Protestantism, the state in most cases, the individual reason in a few, imposes the creed on the church. The king and parliament of Great Britain determine the faith the clergy must profess and maintain; the Protestant princes in Germany have the supreme control of the symbols of the church, the right to enact what creed they please."*

---

* Ante, pp. 17-20.

The revival and general study of the classics, tended by their character to destroy the power of the church of the middle ages, to introduce an order of thought favorable to the supremacy of the civil over the ecclesiastical order, the effect of which is seen in the sudden growth of the monarchical or royal authority, which took place at the close of the fifteenth century, and the beginning of the sixteenth. The influence of this heathen literature, breaking the authority of the church, and the use of fire-arms superseding to some extent the co-operation of the old feudal nobility, combining, enabled the European potentates to shake off the authority of the church, and to establish themselves in their independence. The cause of Protestantism was eminently the cause of the kings, and under the social and political aspect,—the only aspect in which we now consider, or wish to consider the subject at all, —was the cause of the people, only so far as it was for their advantage, to lose the protection of the church, and the feudal noble, and to come under the unrestrained authority of the civil magistrate,— an authority which was not slow to degenerate into unbearable tyranny, as we see in the English revolution in the seventeenth century, and the French in the eighteenth. But fire-arms and classical literature succeeded, by bringing the laity into the literary class, and the commoners into the armies, in breaking down the authority of the church, destroying the old feudal nobility, and in establishing the independence of kings and the temporal governments, and not merely in what were called Protestant countries; for the principle of Protestantism triumphed throughout Europe for a season, in the countries remaining Catholic in name, as well as in those that became avowedly Protestant. Francis I and Charles V would have done what did Henry VIII, the princes of the north of Germany, and Gustavus Adolphus, if they had not humbled the church, and for a time compelled the Holy See to succumb to their interests and wishes.

The independence of civil governments established, and the kings, freed from the dominion of the church and the checks of the old feudal barons, were not slow to adopt a purely worldly policy; and before the close of the fifteenth century, the policy now termed Machiavellian, was adopted and avowed by every court in Europe,—that is to say, a policy wholly detached from all moral and religious doctrines or principles. Machiavelli was born at Florence, of a noble family, in 1469, and, though often execrated, was a great and learned man, and by no means ignorant or destitute of morality. He was *the politician,* the statesman of his epoch, and may be consulted as the highest authority for the maxims on which rested the policy of the European courts at the period under consideration.

3. The invention of printing on movable types, we are far from thinking,—far, very far from wishing to intimate,—is not destined to effect the greatest good; but we are equally decided that, up to the present moment, it would be difficult to say whether it has been productive of the more good or evil. We will not so far dishonor ourselves as even to say that we are the friends of knowledge and universal enlightenment; we know no advocates of ignorance;

we have no sympathy with those, if such there be, who would withhold education from any portion of the human race; but we repeat that we regard half-education as worse than no education. We are not ashamed to avow our agreement with Pope, that

"A little learning is a dangerous thing
Drink deep, or taste not the Pierian spring;
There shallow draughts intoxicate the brain,
But drinking deeply sobers us again."

The great mass of our American people can read and do read the newspapers, and many other things; and all of them fancy themselves competent to sit in judgment on all matters human and divine. They are equal to the profoundest philosophical speculations, the loftiest theological dogmas, and the abstrusest political problems. Filled with a sense of their own wisdom and capacity for sound judgment, they lose all teachableness, and are really in a more deplorable state than if they made no pretensions to general intelligence. Unquestionably we must pass through this stage of superficial knowledge, which merely engenders pride, conceit self-will, before we can come to that of true enlightenment; and therefore we do not complain, but submit to the present evil, consoling ourselves with the hope of the glory hereafter to be revealed. Nevertheless, it is an evil, deny it who will.

Printing, by multiplying books and making the great mass of the people readers, serves to foster the spirit of individualism, which is only one form of supreme selfishness. He who has not the humility to learn, the meekness to obey, who feels that he has no superior, but that he is as good as you, will soon come to feel that he owes no duty but to himself; and that the true morality in his case is to take care of Number One. In this way the invention of printing, co-operating with the causes already mentioned, tended to destroy the church and nobility of the middle ages, to substitute pride, intractableness and egotism for the old spirit of submission and self-denial, and therefore aided on the change we have noted. Ignorance and self-sufficiency pervert Heaven's choicest blessings; and the Bible itself, thrown into the hands of the mass incompetent to its interpretation or right understanding, become, we are often obliged to own, a savor of death unto death, and generates endless sects and interminable strife, as fatal to the cause of piety as to individual and public happiness.

4. On the heels of all this, materialism in philosophy, virtually if not expressly, arrogant individualism in matters of faith, selfishness or a refined or even gross Epicureanism in morals, and the independence and centralization of the civil power in the hands of the absolute monarch, adopting and acting, as Caesar Borgia and Ferdinand of Aragon, on a policy wholly detached from religion and morality, came the discovery of the passage round the Cape of Good Hope, and of this Western Continent. Already had men's minds been drawn off from high spiritual subjects; already had they begun to be heathenized, and of the earth earthy; the church was reduced to be a tool of the state; the minister of religion shorn of his sacred authority and converted into a police officer. The world was ripe for a new order of things; for entering into the career of industrial aggrandizement, the

accumulation of treasures on earth, forgetful that moth and rust may corrupt and thieves break through and steal. The newly discovered worlds afforded the means both of increasing and of satisfying this tendency. A sudden change came over the whole industrial world; visions of untold wealth floated before all eyes; and men who would in the twelfth century have been content to lead lives of self-denial, and to labor as peaceful monks, seeking in their quiet retreats for the crown of God's approval, were crossing all oceans, penetrating into all forests, digging into all mountains, in pursuit of GOLD. The love of gold supplanted the love of God; and the professed followers of Christ no longer made pilgrimages to the Holy Land, but to the Gold Coast, to Florida, Mexico, and Peru, in pursuit not of the sacred relics of saints and martyrs, monuments consecrated by faith and love, but of the fabled Eldorado. Commerce took a new flight, and in a few years manufactures began to flourish, great industrial establishments to spring up; science and inventive genius came in— Manchester, Leeds, Lowell,—an immense operative population wanting shirts to their backs while shirts are lying idle, piled up in warehouses, and they starving in the midst of abundance!

We have here glanced at some of the causes which have operated to destroy the religious faith of the middle ages, to abolish the worship of God in Christian lands, and to introduce the worship of Mammon, —all-triumphant Mammon. Going along through the streets of Boston the other day, we remarked that it has become the fashion to convert the basement floors of our churches into retail shops of various

kinds of merchandise. How significant! The church
is made to rest on TRADE; Christ on Mammon.
Was any thing ever more typical? The rents of these
shops in some cases, we are told, pay the whole expense of the minister's salary. Poor minister! if thou
shouldst but take it into thy head to rebuke Mammon, as thy duty bids thee, and to point out the
selfishness and iniquity of the dominant spirit of
trade, thy underpinning would slide from under thee,
and thou wouldst- - - - . But land is valuable; and
why should it lie idle all days in the week but one,
because a meeting-house stands on it? Ay, sure
enough. O, blessed thrift, great art thou, and hast
learned to coin thy God and to put him out at usury!
But what hast thou gained? Thou are care-worn
and haggard, and with all thy economies, begrudging
Heaven the small plat of ground for his temple,—
Heaven who gives thee all, this whole earth, so much
broader than thou canst cultivate, thou hast to provide bread and soup societies for the poor starving
men and women, who would work, but can get no
work.

Here we are, in Ireland, every third person reduced to live on third-rate potatoes, these scantily
obtained, and for only thirty-six weeks in the year;
in England and Scotland, with dark lanes, Stockport cellars, and St. Ives work-houses, Manchester
insurrections, gloomy enough; in France, no great
better, daily *émeutes*, kept down by sheer force of
armed soldiery; and in this country, following rapidly
on in the same way, godless and heartless, sneering
at virtue, philanthropy, owning no relation of man
to man but what Carlyle terms "cash payment."

What is to be the upshot of all this? Dear countrymen, we have before to-day told you all this; but
though you are wise, intelligent, virtuous—the freest,
noblest, meekest, humblest people that ever breathed
this blessed air of heaven, we see nothing that you
are doing to guard against worse, or to remedy what
is bad. We read the newspapers, the protecting
genii and guardian angels of the land. We seize the
leading editorials, and in the simplicity of our heart
and the eagerness of our spirit ask, What cheer?
Surely, with so many Able Editors, all toiling and
sweating at the anvil, all devoted heart and soul to
the public good, we must be safe, and the means
of averting the calamity dreaded must be within our
reach; the remedy must be found out and insisted
on. Alas! brother editors, we love and honor you;
but we must say, we see not as ye touch the problem,
conceive of it even, far less propose a solution. Ye
are all at work with details, with petty schemes,
proposing nothing that comes up to the mark. Some
of you talk of Home Industry; the wisest among
you talk of Free Trade; none of you, as we hear,
speak of God, and tell your readers that for a people
who worship Mammon, there is no good. Nay, you
must not speak of these matters; for if you do, who
will advertise in your columns or subscribe for your
papers? Nay, how many subscribers will our friend,
the Editor of this Journal, lose by inserting this
very Article? Are we not trenching at every moment
on forbidden ground? Do we say one word that
party leaders will not turn pale or look cross at?
What political capital can be made out of what we
say? Alas! brother editors, do not think we intend

to upbraid you. God knows our condition is not one to be envied. With the whole weight of the republic on our shoulders, and we, alas! none of the strongest in bone or muscle! God pity us! For to carry this huge republic, with its Mammon worships, and its Christian churches reared on traders' shops, and its party strifes, its rush for office, its forgetfulness of man's brotherhood to man, its morality of Let us alone, Save who can, and the devil take the hindmost; workers no longer finding work to do; master-workers counting their obligations to their workmen discharged in full when the stipulated wages are paid; it is no easy matter.

But, after all, what is the remedy? Let us not deceive ourselves. The whole head is sick, the whole heart is faint. Our industrial arrangements, the relations of master-workers, and workers, of capital and labor, which have grown up during these last three hundred years, are essentially vicious, and, as we have seen, are beginning throughout Christendom to prove themselves so. The great evil is not now in the tyranny or oppression of governments as such; it is not in the arbitrary power of monarchies, aristocracies, or democracies; but it is in the heart of the people, and the industrial order. It is simply, under the industrial head, so far as concerns our material well-being, in this fact, this mournful fact, that there is no longer any certainty of the born worker obtaining always work whereby he can provide for the ordinary wants of a human being. Nor is this altogether the fault of the master-workers. To a very great extent, the immediate employer is himself in turn employed; and as all who produce,

produce to sell, their means of employing, constantly and at reasonable wages, evidently depend on the state of the market; workmen must, therefore, with every depression of trade, be thrown out of employment, whatever the benevolence of the master-workers.

Nor is it possible, with the present organization, or rather *dis*organization of industry, to prevent these ruinous fluctuations of trade. They may undoubtedly be exaggerated by bad legislation, as they may be mitigated by wise and just administration of government, but prevented altogether they cannot be. For this plain reason, that more can be produced, in any given year, with the present productive power, than can be sold in any given five years,—we mean sold to the actual consumer. In other words, by our vicious method of distributing the products of labor, we destroy the possibility of keeping up an equilibrium between production and consumption. We create a surplus—that is a surplus, not when we consider the wants of the people, but when we consider the state of the markets—and then must slacken our hands till the surplus is worked off. During this time, while we are working off the surplus while the mills run short time, or stop altogether, the workmen must want employment. The evil is inherent in the system. We say it is inherent in the *system of wages,* of cash payments, which, as at present understood, the world has for the first time made any general experiment of only now, since the Protestant reformation.

Let us not be misinterpreted. We repeat not here the folly of some men about equality, and every man being in all things his own guide and master. This world is not so made. There must be in all branches of human activity, mental, social, industrial, chiefs and leaders. Rarely, if ever, does a man remain a workman at wages, who could succeed in managing an industrial establishment for himself. Here is our friend Mr. Smith, an excellent hatter, kind-hearted, charitable, and succeeds well; but of the fifty hands he employs, not one could take his place. Many of these journeymen of his have been in business for themselves, but failed. They are admirable workmen, but have not the capacity to direct, to manage, to carry on business. It is so the world over. There must be chiefs in religion, in politics, in industry; the few must lead, the many must follow. This is the order of nature; it is the ordinance of God; and it is worse than idle to contend against it. The great question concerns the mode of designating these chiefs, and the form of the relation which shall subsist between them and the rest of the community. Our present mode of designating them in the industrial world—in the political we manage it in this country somewhat better—is obviously defective, and the relation expressed by wages, in our modern sense of the term, is an undeniable failure. Under it there is no security, no permanency, no true prosperity, for either worker or master-worker; both hurry on to one common ruin.

This, we are well aware, will not be believed. We do not believe ourselves ill. We mistake the hectic flush on the cheek for the hue of health. "We have heard," say our readers, "this cry of ruin ever since we could remember, and yet we have gone on pros-

pering, increasing in wealth, refinement, art, literature, science, and doubling our population every
thirty years." Yes, and we shall continue to prosper
in the same way. The present stagnation of trade will
last not much longer; business will soon revive, nay,
is reviving; and we shall feel that the evil day is too
far off to be guarded against. We shall grow richer;
we shall build up yet larger industries; the hammer
will ring from morning till night—till far into the
night; the clack of the cotton-mill will accompany
the music of every waterfall; the whole land be covered by a vast network of railroads and canals; our
ships will display their canvas upon every sea, and
fill every port; our empire shall extend from the At-
lantic to the Pacific, and from the Northern Ocean to
the Isthmus of Darien; we shall surpass England as
much as ancient Carthage surpassed the mother
Phoenicia; be the richest, the most renowned nation
the world ever saw. All this, it needs no prophetic
eye to foresee; prosperity of this sort we may have,
shall have. It is not of outward, material ruin we
speak. But what will avail all this outward prosperity,—our industries, our wealth, our arts, our lux-
uries, our boundless empire, our millions of people,
if we contain in our midst a greater mass of corruption, of selfishness, of vice, of crime, of abject misery
and wretchedness, than the world ever saw before?
And yet, such will be our fate if we continue on in
the path, nay, the broad road, in which we are now
travelling.

But once more, we are asked, what is the remedy?
Shall we go back to the middle ages, to feudalism
and the old Catholic church? No, dear countrymen,

no. This is no longer possible even if it were desirable. We have got firearms, heathen literature, printing, and the new world; with these it is not possible to reconstruct the middle ages. How often must we remind you that there is no going back? Who ever knew yesterday to return? From the bottom of our heart we believe these much decried middle ages were far preferable,—regarded as definitive,—to our own. What we have as yet obtained by departing from them,—unless we make it the stepping-stone to something more,—is far beneath them. The Israelites in the wilderness, we must needs believe were,— saving the hope of reaching the promised land,— worse off than in Egypt making bricks for their taskmasters; but this promised land, flowing with milk and honey, lay *before* them, not behind them, and could be reached not by returning to Egypt, but by pressing *onward through* the wilderness. We pray thee, gentle, or rather *un*gentle reader, not to misinterpret us, on this point, as thou art wont to do. No more than thou dost do we believe in the perfection of the middle ages, as much as we may admire them, and as much superior to the present as we certainly hold them. We would not bring them back if we could. They do not come up to our ideal of what is most desirable for the human race; nor to what is attainable even. They had many and heavy drawbacks. Out from under the veil of romance, which time and genius have woven for them, we see ever and anon the ghastly death's head peering. No wise man regrets their departure; no wise man labors to reproduce them; and herein the Schlegels and Oxford divines are not wise, and do but kick against the pricks. We grieve not that we can have these ages no more; that feudalism is gone, and the church of Gregory VII, that Napoleon of the ecclesiastical order, is gone, never to return; but we do grieve that in getting rid of them, we have supplied their place by nothing better; by nothing so good. In contrasting them with the present, we have wished to show our countrymen that they should not be contented with the present, nor despair of something better; for better once was and may be again; though not in the old form.

But if we would not reconstruct the old feudal and Catholic society, we would have what feudalism and mediæval Catholicity sought to realize; and to some extent, though in a rude and imperfect manner, it may be, *did* realize. We would have men *governed,* and well governed, let who will be the governors, or what form adopted there may be for selecting them. God's curse and humanity's curse also do and will rest on the no-government schemers. Satan himself was chief anarch, and all anarchs are his children. Men need government, nay, have a *right* to demand government, without which there is no life for them. We would also see revived in all its mediæval force and activity the Christian faith, and as the interpreter of that faith, the Christian church, one and indivisible; the ground and pillar of the truth; clothed with the authority which of right belongs to it; and enjoining and exercising a discipline on high and low, rich and poor, as effective as that of the middle ages, but modified to meet the new wants and relations of Christendom. There is no true *living* on this God's earth, for men who do not believe in God, in Christ,

in the ever present spirit of truth, justice, love; in
the reality of the spiritual world; nor without the
church of Christ, active and efficient, authoritative
over faith and conscience, competent to instruct us in
the mysteries of our destiny, and to direct us wisely
and surely through the creation of a heaven here on
earth, to a holier and higher heaven hereafter. We
must revoke the divorce unwisely and wickedly de-
creed between politics and religion and morality.
It must not be accounted a superfluity in the politician to have a conscience; nor an impertinence to
speak and to act as if he believed in the eternal
God, and feared the retributions of the unseen world;
nor inconsistent with the acknowledged duties of
the minister of religion, to withhold absolution from
the base politician, the foul wretch, whatever his private morals, who will in public life betray his country, or support an unjust policy through plea of
utility or mere expediency. It must not always be in
vain that a public measure is shown to be unjust in
order to secure its defeat, or just, in order to secure
its adoption. Nations must be made to feel that there
is a Higher than they, and that they may lawfully do
only what the Sovereign of sovereigns commands.
Right must be carried into the cabinet councils of
ministers, into legislative halls, into the bureaus of
business, and preside at the tribunals of justice; men
must be made to feel deep in their inmost being,
whether in public life or in private life, that they are
watched by the all-seeing Eye, and that it is better to
be poor, better to beg, better to starve, than to de-
part in the least iota from the law of rigid justice,
and thrice blessed charity. This is what we need;

what we *demand* for our country, for all countries; and demand too in the reverend name of him who was, and is, and is to be, and in the sacred name of humanity, whose maternal heart is wounded by the least wound received by the least significant of her children.

But how shall this faith be reproduced? It is not for us to answer this question. There are, as we compute, some fifteen thousand clergymen in this country, of all names and grades; all, we are bound to presume, good men and true; apostolic men; laboring with an eye single to the glory of their Master in the salvation of men; able ministers of the New Testament, comprehending all mysteries, and competent to unfold to us the destinies of man and society; speaking with an unction from the Holy One, words of truth with power, as men having authority. To these belongs the prerogative to answer the question proposed. We have no disposition to encroach on their peculiar province. But, holy fathers, permit us with all respect for your order, to ask, you being what we have presumed, how happens it that truth dies out of the hearts of the people, that God's altars are everywhere digged down, and those of Mammon set up? It is not for us to rebuke an elder, but, holy fathers, does not this fact speak of neglected duty, of unfaithfulness to your charge? Your profession falls into disrepute; your flocks run after strange gods, and set up those to be gods which are no gods. Some of your most zealous supporters, who are severest against those who reverence you not, who carry around the box of charity, put a penny in but do take a shilling out;

your well dressed hearers, in their soft cushioned pews, smile or sleep when you talk of heaven, of hell, of eternity, of man's accountability and the necessity of seeking heaven by self-denial, by crucifying the world, and exercising faith towards God and charity towards men. These old-fashioned notions seem to be outgrown, and men fancy themselves now gliding on safely to the Celestial City, as our friend Hawthorne has it, on recently constructed railroads, with Apollyon himself for conductor and chief engineer. Could this have happened, holy fathers, if you had been faithful to the great Head of the church? O, it is a fearful thing that you and we shall be compelled to answer at the dread tribunal for the faith of this people! God will ask of us, Where are the children I committed to your charge? What shall we have to answer?

Politically, also, we need something, and something may unquestionably be done, especially in this country where the people are supreme, inasmuch as the people are wise and virtuous. Were it our province to suggest any thing to be done under this head, we should recommend the complete destruction of the paper-money system, the repeal of all measures facetiously called protection of home industry, which tax one interest for the purpose of building up another, and labor for the enhancement of the profits of capital; and the adoption of a uniform measure of values, so that men shall buy and sell by the same measure, and trade cease to be only a respectable form of gambling with loaded dice. But, we are told that the great merit of the politician is to find out and conform to the will of the people;

we will therefore make no proposition. There are at least in this country, computing federal and state officers, from president down to tide-waiters, and governors down to field-drivers, all told, not less than one hundred and fifty thousand office-holders, to say nothing of twice as many office-seekers, hardly if at all their inferiors. These are the political chiefs of the people. The people are virtuous and intelligent. They will always therefore select the most virtuous and intelligent of their number for their chiefs. These office-holders, therefore, are and must be held to be a fair and full representation of the virtue and intelligence of the American people.

Now, it belongs to these, the selected chiefs of the people, to introduce and carry through all needed political reforms. Political Chiefs, you are intrusted with power; you have the confidence of the people; you are selected by us to be our governors and guides. Now, in the name of our common country we call upon you, since you unquestionably have the ability, to put an end to the evils we have complained of, so far as they belong to your department. We are sure the people, if they are as wise and as virtuous as you tell them they are, and have made them believe they are, have never wished the political state of things which now is. We are sure, that the great mass of your constituents, however they may err as to means, do really prefer good government, which maintains freedom for all, and which at least gives us this simple kind of liberty of which Carlyle speaks, to buy where we can cheapest, to sell where dearest. Do you then regard this will, resign your functions, or work out something better than we now have; and better not merely for rich capitalists and trading politicians, but better for our poor sister the washerwoman, and the still poorer sister, the sempstress, with her three little children growing up in ignorance, to be corrupted by the rabble rout with which they must associate.

Of industrial reforms properly so called, we speak not. Owenisms, Saint-Simonisms, Fourierisms, Communisms, and *isms* enough in all conscience are rife, indicating at least, that men are beginning to feel that the present industrial relations are becoming quite unbearable. Three years ago, we brought forward our "Morrison Pill," but the public made up wry faces, and absolutely refused to take it; so much the worse for them. We cannot afford to throw away our medicines, even if they are quack medicines. We cease attempting to prescribe. We leave this matter to the natural chiefs of industry, that is, to bank presidents, cashiers, and directors; to the presidents and directors of insurance offices, of railroads and other corporations; heavy manufacturers, and leading merchants; the master-workers, in Carlyle's terminology, the Plugsons of Undershot. Messrs. Plugsons of Undershot, you are a numerous and a powerful body. You are the chiefs of industry, and in some sort hold our lives in your pockets. You are a respectable body. We see you occupying the chief seats in the synagogues, consulted by secretaries of the treasury, constituting boards of trade, conventions of manufacturers, forming home leagues, presiding over lyceums, making speeches at meetings for the relief of the poor, and other charitable purposes. You are great; you are respectable; and you have a benevolent regard for all poor laborers. Suffer us, alas! a poor laborer enough, to do you homage, and render you the tribute of our gratitude. Think not that we mean to reproach you with the present state of industry and the working men. We have no reproaches to bring. But, ye are able to place our industry on its right basis, and we call upon you to do it; nay, we tell you that not we only, but a Higher than any of us, will hold you responsible for the *future* condition of the industrial classes. If you govern industry only with a view to your own profit, to the profit of master-workers, we tell you that the little you contribute to build work-houses, and to furnish bread and soup, will not be held as a final discharge. If God has given you capacities to lead, it has been that you might be a blessing to those who want that capacity. As he will hold the clergy responsible for the religious faith of the people, as he will hold the political chiefs responsible for the wise ordinance and administration of government, so, respected Masters, will he hold you responsible for the wise organization of industry and the just distribution of its fruits. Here, we dare speak, for here we are the interpreter of the law of God. Every pang the poor mother feels over her starving boy, is recorded in heaven against you, and goes to swell the account you are running up there, and which you, with all your *financiering,* may be unable to discharge. Do not believe that no books are kept but your own, nor that your method of book-keeping by double entry is the highest method, the most perfect. Look to it, then. What does it profit, though a man gain the whole world and lose his own soul?

Ay, respected Masters, as little as ye think of the matter, ye have souls, and souls that can be *lost*, too, if not lost already. In God's name, in humanity's name, nay, in the name of your own souls, which will not relish the fire that is never quenched, nor feel at ease under the gnawings of the worm that never dies, let us entreat you to lose no time in re-arranging industry, and preventing the recurrence of these evils, which with no malice we have roughly sketched for you to look upon. The matter, friends, is pressing, and delay may prove fatal. Remember, there is a God in heaven, who may say to you, "Go to now, ye rich men, weep and howl for your miseries that shall come upon you; your riches are corrupted, and your garments are moth-eaten, your gold and silver is cankered; and the rust of them shall be a witness against you, and shall eat your flesh as it were fire. You have stored up to yourselves wrath against the last days. Behold the hire of the laborers who have reaped your fields of which you have defrauded them, crieth out; and the cry of them hath entered into the ears of the Lord of Sabaoth." This is not our denunciation; it is not the declamation of the agrarian seeking to arm the poor against the rich; but it is God himself speaking to you now in warning, what he will hereafter, unless you are wise, speak to you in retribution.

CHAPTER TWO

SOCIALISM AND THE CHURCH*

NOTE ON "SOCIALISM AND THE CHURCH"

When this essay appeared in *Brownson's Quarterly Review* (January, 1849), the Communist Manifesto was only a few months old, and the great states of Europe were bleeding from the revolutionary frenzy of the previous year. Metternich had fallen at last, and the fountains of the great deep seemed broken up; only Britain and America felt reasonably secure from violence. Brownson, himself among the most vigorous and sincere American radicals only a few years before, now undertook the defense of traditional establishments against Marxism, and exposed socialism for a degraded caricature of Christianity. "Socialism, by its very principle, enslaves us to nature and society, and subjects us to all the fluctuations of time and sense." In this article, Brownson expounds the Christian doctrine of resignation with a strong pathos.

*　　*　　*

[From *Brownson's Quarterly Review* for January, 1849.]

This handsomely printed volume has been sent us "from the author," and we can do no less than acknowledge its reception. It is filled with the wild speculations and demoralizing theories hardly to be expected from "a Woman." In a literary point of view, it is beneath criticism, but it bears the marks of some reading, and even of hard, though ill-direct-

---

* *England the Civilizer; her History developed in its Principles; with Reference to the Civilizational History of Modern Europe (America inclusive), and with a View to the Dénouement of the Difficulties of the Hour.* By a Woman. London: 1848.

ed, thinking. Nature has treated the author liberally, and she will have much to answer for. The work could have proceeded only from a strong mind and a corrupt heart.

The work itself pertains to the socialistic school, and, substantially, to the Fourieristic section of that school. According to it, the human race began its career in ignorance and weakness, and established a false system of civilization. Modern society, dating from the fall of the western Roman Empire, has been engaged in a continual struggle to throw off that system, and to establish a true system in its place. It has been engaged, thus far, in the work of demolition, which it has finally terminated. It has prepared the ground for true civilization, and the human race now stand waiting, or did stand waiting on the first of January, 1848, the signal to introduce it, and to put an end for ever to all evils, moral, social, and physical.

The old civilization, now effete, committed the capital error of recognizing religion,—in the language of the author, *superstition,*—government, property, and "the ascendency of the male sex," or family,—for the family cannot subsist without that ascendency;—the new civilization will correct this error, and for religion substitute science; for government, federation; for law, instinct; for property, communal wealth; for family, love; and for the ascendency of the male sex, the administration of women. Consequently, the new civilization is to be a petticoat civilization, in which we must include the human race in those genera which are named after the female, as cows, geese, ducks, hens, &c.

Into the details of this new civilization, or the means by which it is to be introduced and preserved, we need not enter. Some things may be assumed to be settled; if not, the human race can settle nothing, and it is idle to examine the claims of a new theory. If any thing can be settled, it is that the man is the head of the woman,—that she is for him, not he for her; and that religion, government, family, property, are essential elements of all civilization. Without them man must sink below the savage, for in the lowest savage state we find, at least, some reminiscences of them. Any system which proposes their abolition or essential modification is by that fact alone condemned, and proved to deserve no examination. We do the socialists too much honor when we consent to hear and refute their dreams. We have not at this late day to resettle the basis of society, to seek for unknown truth in religion or politics, in relation to public or domestic, private or social life; we have no new discoveries to make, no important changes to introduce; and all that we need attempt is to ascertain the truth which has been known from the beginning, and to conform ourselves to it.

Nevertheless, the work before us is a pregnant sign of the times, and may afford food for much useful reflection to those prepared to digest it. People who attend to their own business, tread the routine their fathers trod, and attempt to discharge in peace and quiet the practical duties of their state, little suspect what is fermenting in the heated brains of this nineteenth century. They know next to nothing of what is going on around them. They look upon the doctrines contained in works like the one before us as the speculations of a few insane dreamers, and are sure that the good sense of mankind will prevent them from spreading, and confine their mischief to the misguided individuals who put them forth. They regard them as too ridiculous, as too absurd, to be believed. They can do no harm, and we need not trouble our heads about them. This is certainly a plausible view of the subject, but, unhappily, there is nothing too ridiculous or too absurd to be believed, if demanded by the dominant spirit or sentiment of an age or country; for what is seen to be demanded by that spirit or sentiment never appears ridiculous or absurd to those who are under its influence.

Nothing, to a rightly instructed mind, is more ridiculous or absurd than the infidelity which so extensively prevailed in the last century, and which under another form prevails equally in this. Yet when the philosophy which necessarily implied it first made its appearance, few comparatively took the alarm, and even learned and sound churchmen were unable to persuade themselves that there was any serious danger to be apprehended. When the philosophers and literary men went further, and, developing that philosophy, actually made free with the Scriptures, and even the mysteries of faith, the majority of those who should have seen what was coming paid little attention to them, jested at the incipient incredulity with great good humor, felt sure that no considerable number of persons would proceed so far as to deny not only the church, but the very existence of God, and flattered themselves that the infidelity which was manifest would prove only a temporary fashion, a momentary caprice, which would soon become weary of itself, and evaporate. Nevertheless, all the while, the age was virtually infidel, and thousands of those who had persisted in believing there was no danger were themselves but shortly after driven into exile, or brought to the guillotine by its representatives. The same thing occurs now in regard to socialism. The great body of those who have faith and sound principles look upon it as the dream of a few isolated individuals, as undeserving a moment's attention, and think it a waste of time and breath even to caution the public against it. Yet in one form or other it has already taken possession of the age, has armed itself for battle, made the streets of Paris, Berlin, Frankfort, Vienna, and other cities, run with blood, and convulsed nearly the whole civilized world. It is organized all through Europe and the United States; scarcely a book, a tract, or a newspaper is issued from a constantly teeming press, that does not favor it, and there is scarcely any thing else going that can raise a shout of applause from the people; and yet we are told, even by grave men, that it is a matter which need excite no apprehension.

Nor is this the worst aspect of the case. Not a few of those who shrink with horror from socialism, as drawn out and set forth by its avowed advocates, do themselves, unconsciously, adopt and defend the very principles of which it is only the logical development; nay, not only adopt and defend those principles, but denounce, as behind their age, as the enemies of the people, those who call them in question. Have we not ourselves been so denounced? If you doubt it, read the criticisms of *The Boston Pilot* on our review of Padre Ventura's *Oration,* or *The New York Commercial Advertiser's* notice of our censure of the Italian Liberals for their persecution of the Jesuits. Of course, these papers have no authority of their own, but they echo public opinion, and tell, as well as straws, which way the wind blows. If the public condemned in no measured terms the "horrible doctrines" we a few years since put forth in an *Essay on the Laboring Classes,* it has not condemned, but through some of its leading organs commended, an article on *The Distribution of Property,* published in *The North American Review* for July, 1848, the most conservative periodical, except our own, in the country,—which defends at length, and with more ability than we ordinarily expect in that Journal, the very principles from which we logically derived them. We hold now in utter detestation the doctrines of the Essay referred to and which raised a terrible c l a m o r against us throughout the country; but we proved, in our defence, and no one has yet, to our knowledge, ventured to maintain the contrary, that those doctrines were only legitimate conclusions from the Protestant and democratic premises held by the great body of our countrymen, and by what they do and must regard as the more enlightened portion of mankind. In fact, a very common objection to us was, that we were ahead of the age, that is, drew the conclusions before the people were ready to receive them. We did but reason logically from the principles we had imbibed from public opinion, from general literature, and the practical teachings of those we had been accustomed from our childhood to hear mentioned with honor, and had been required to revere, —principles, which we had never heard questioned, and never thought of questioning, till we undertook to explain to ourselves the universal outcry which had been raised against us. As we found our countrymen saying two and two, we thought we might innocently add, two and two *make four,* and complete the proposition. We were wrong, not in our logic, but in our principles. We had trusted the age; we had confided in its maxims, and received them as axioms. As the mists cleared away, as the gloss of novelty wore off, and the excitement of self-defence subsided, we saw the horrible nature of the doctrines we had put forth, and recoiled, not only from them, but from the principles of which they were the necessary logical development. But the age has not followed our example. The great body of the people continue to adhere to those principles, and will not suffer them to be questioned.

No doubt, the majority of numbers are as yet unprepared to adopt socialism as developed by Owen, Fourier, Saint-Simon, Cabet, Proudhon, or by "A Woman" in the work before us; but no man who has studied the age can, if he have any tolerable powers of generalization, doubt that socialistic principles are those now all but universally adopted. They are at the bottom of nearly all hearts, and at work in nearly all minds; and just in proportion as men acquire courage enough to say not only two and two, two and two, but that two and two *make four,* the age rushes to their practical realization,—accepts their logical developments, however horrible, however impious. There is an invincible logic in society which pushes it to the realization of the last consequences of its principles. In vain do moderate men cry out against carrying matters to extremes; in vain do practical men appeal to common sense; in vain do brave men rush before the movement and with their bodies attempt to interpose a barrier to its onward progress. Society no more—nay, less— than individuals recoils from the conclusions which follow logically from premises it holds to be sound and well established. It draws practically those conclusions, with a terrible earnestness, and a despotism that scorns every limitation. On it moves, heedless of what or of whom it may crush beneath the wheels of its ponderous car. Woe to him who seeks to stay its movement! Social evils grow as it advances, and these it lays to the charge of those who would hold it back, and result, it maintains, only from the fact that it has not yet reached its goal. The reform is not carried far enough. Put on more steam, carry it further, carry it further, is the loud cry it raises.

We see this in the Protestant reformation. The reformers did not fulfil their promises, did not secure to the people the good they had led them to expect. Everybody saw this, everybody felt it; for everybody found himself distracted and unsatisfied. What was the inference drawn? That the reformers had erred in principle, and that the reformation could not secure the good promised? By no means. The people had accepted its principles. The reform, said they, is good, is just and true; but it has not been carried far enough; the reformers were only half reformed; they stopped short of the mark. The reform must not stop with Luther and Calvin; we must carry it further. This is what the children of the reformation said, as we all know; and they have been from the first struggling to carry it further and further, and have at length carried it to the borders, if not into the regions, of nihility. The evils remain, nay, every day increase, and each day a new party rises up in the bosom of the most advanced sect, and demands a further advance.

In the political world we see the same thing. Revolution has followed revolution, and no political reform goes far enough to satisfy its friends. In the last century, revolutions were *political,* and had for their object the establishment of political equality, or democracy. It was soon seen that political equality answers no purpose where there is *social* inequality. A writer, who could speak with as much authority on this subject as any of our contemporaries, thus expressed himself in 1841:—

"But democracy as a form of government, *political* democracy, as we call it, could not be the term of popular aspiration. Regarded in itself, without reference to any thing ulterior, it is no better than the aristocratic form of government, or even the monarchical. Universal suffrage and eligibility, the expression of perfect equality before the state, and which with us are nearly realized, unless viewed as means to an end, are not worth contending for. What avails it, that all men are equal before the state, if they must stop there? If under a democracy, aside from mere politics, men may be as unequal in their social conditions as under other forms of government, wherein consist the boasted advantages of your democracy? Is all possible good summed up in suffrage and eligibility? Is the millennium realized, when every man may vote and be voted for? Yet this is all that political democracy, reduced to its simplest elements, proposes. Political democracy, then, can never satisfy the popular mind. This democracy is only one step—a necessary step—in its progress. Having realized equality before the state, the popular mind passes naturally to equality before society. It seeks and accepts *political* democracy only as a means to *social* democracy; and it cannot fail to attempt to realize equality in men's social condition, when it has once realized equality in their political condition."—*The Boston Quarterly Review,* January, 1841, pp. 113, 114.

Political democracy leaves the principal social evils unredressed, and the causes which led the reform thus far remain in all their force to carry it still further. Hence we see in the present century the same party which in the last demanded political democracy attempting throughout nearly the whole civilized world a series of revolutions in favor of social democracy. The leaders in the late French revolution tell you that it was a social revolution they sought, and that it was this fact which distinguished it from the revolution of 1789. In Italy and Germany two revolutions are going on at once, a political revolution and a social revolution. Young Italy is socialistic; so is Young Germany; and it was its socialistic character that gave to the movement of Ronge and his associates its significance and its moderate success. The race, modern philosophers tell us, is progressive, and in a certain sense we concede it. It tends invariably to reach the end implied in the principles it adopts or the impulse it has received, and that tendency is never self-arrested. Its progress towards that end is irresistible; and when it happens to be downward, as at present, it is fearfully rapid, and becomes more fearfully rapid in proportion to the distance it descends.

The only possible remedy is, not declamation against the horrible results, the pernicious conclusions, at which the popular mind arrives,—the resource of weak men,—but the correction of the popular premises and recalling the people to sound first principles. Once concede that even political equality is a good, and object worth seeking, you must concede that social equality is also a good; and social equality is necessarily the annihilation of religion, government, property, and family. The same principle which would justify the Moderate Republicans of France in dethroning the king would justify M. Proudhon in making war on property, declaring every rich man a robber, and seeking to exterminate the *bourgeoisie,* as these have already exterminated the nobility. There is no stopping-place between legitimacy—whether monarchical or republican legitimacy—and the most ultra socialism. Once in the career of political reform,—we say *political,* not *administrative,* reform,—we are pledged to pursue it to its last results. We are miserable cowards, or worse, if we shrink from the legitimate deductions from our own premises. There is not a meaner sin than the sin of inconsequence,—a sin against our own rational nature which distinguishes us from the mere animal world. If we adopt the socialistic premises, we must go on with the socialists in their career of destruction; nay, we shall be compelled to do so, or strew the battle-field with our dead bodies. If we recoil from the socialistic conclusions, we must re-examine our own premises, and reject distinctly, unreservedly, and heroically every socialistic principle we may have unwittingly adopted, every socialistic tendency we may have unintentionally cherished.

The people, it is well known, do not discriminate, do not perceive, until it is too late, the real nature and tendency of their principles. They mix up truth and falsehood, and can hardly ever be made to distinguish the one from the other. They adopt principles which appear to them sound and wholesome, and which under a certain aspect are so, and, unconscious of aiming at what is destructive, they place no confidence in any who tell them they expose themselves to danger. They see no connection between their principles and the conclusions against which we warn them, and which they at present, as well as we, perhaps view with horror; they therefore conclude that the connection we assert is purely imaginary, that we ourselves are deceived, or have some sinister purpose in asserting it; that we are wedded to the past, in love with old abuses, because, perhaps, we profit, or hope to profit, by them; that we do not understand our age, are narrow and contracted in our views, with no love or respect for the poorest and most numerous class. In a word, they set us down as rank conservatives or aristocrats. No age ever comprehends itself, and the people, following its dominant spirit, can never give an account of their own principles. They never trace them out to their last results, and are unable to follow the chain of reasoning by which horrible consequences are linked to premises which appear to them innocent. They never see whither they are going. Democratic philosophers themselves tell us as much, and defend their doctrine on the ground that the people are directed by divine instincts and obey a wisdom which is not their own. To this effect we may quote the writer already cited, and who, on this point, was among the more moderate of his class.

"Philosophy," he says, "is not needed by the masses; but they who separate themselves from the masses, and who believe that the masses are entirely dependent on them for truth and virtue, need it, in order to bring them back and bind them again to universal Humanity. And they need it now, and in this country, perhaps, as much as ever. The world is filled with commotions. The masses are heaving and rolling, like a mighty river, swollen with recent rains, and snows dissolving on the mountains, onward to a distant and unknown ocean. There are those among us, who stand awe-struck, who stand amazed. What means this heaving and onward rolling? Whither tend these mighty masses of human beings? Will they sweep away every fixture, every house and barn, every mark of civilization? Where will they end? In what will they end? Shall we rush before them and attempt to stay their progress? Or shall we fall into their ranks and on with them to their goal? 'Fall into their ranks; be not afraid; be not startled; *a divine instinct guides and moves onward that heaving and rolling mass;* and lawless and destructive as it may seem to you, ye onlookers, it is normal and holy, pursuing a straight and harmless direction on to the union of Man with God.' So answers philosophy, and this is its glory. The friends of humanity need philosophy, as the means of legitimating the cause of the people, of proving that it is the right, and the duty, of every man to bind himself to that cause, and to maintain it in good report and in evil report, in life and in death. They need it, that they may prove to these conservatives, who are frightened almost out of their wits at the movements of the masses, and who are denouncing them in no measured terms, that these movements are from God, and that they who war against them are warring against truth, duty, God, and Humanity. They need it, that they may no longer be obliged to make apologies for their devotion to the masses, their democratic sympathies and tendencies. They who are persecuted for righteousness' sake, who are loaded with reproach for their fidelity to truth and duty, who are all but cast out of the pale of Humanity, because they see, love and pursue Humanity's true interests,—they need it, that they may comprehend the cause of the opposition they meet, forgive their enemies, silence the gainsayer and give to him that asks it a reason for the hope that is in them. The friends of progress, here and everywhere, need it, that, having vindicated, legitimated progress, as philosophers, they may go into the saloons, the universities, the halls of legislation, the pulpit, and abroad among the people, and preach it, with the dignity and the authority of the prophet."—*The Boston Quarterly Review,* January, 1838, pp. 104, 105.

It is necessary to take this ground, or give up democracy, which Mr. Bancroft defines "Eternal Justice ruling through the people," as wholly indefensible; for it cannot be denied that popular movements are blind, and that in them the people are borne onward whither they see not, and by a force they comprehend not. Hence it is easy to understand, that, retaining in their memories traces of former instructions, they may recoil with horror from the last consequences of socialism, and yet be intent only on developing socialistic tendencies, and crushing all opposition to them.

Socialism is, morever, presented in a form admirably adapted to deceive the people, and to secure their support. It comes in Christian guise, and seeks to express itself in the language of the Gospel. Men whom this age delights to honor have called our blessed Lord "the Father of Democracy," and not few or insignificant are those who tell us that he was "the first socialist." In this country, the late Dr. Channing took the lead in reducing the Gospel to socialism; and in France, the now fallen Abbé de La Mennais, condemned by Gregory XVI, of immortal memory, was the first, we believe, who labored to establish the identity of socialism and Christianity. We gave in another place, in 1840, a brief notice of his views on this point, which it may not be uninstructive to reproduce:

"The most remarkable feature in the Abbé de La Mennais's doctrine of liberty is its connection with religion. It is well known, that for some time the friends of freedom in Europe have been opposed to the church, and in general to all religion. The privileged orders have also taken great pains to make it widely believed, that religion requires the support of existing abuses, and that no one can contend for social meliorations without falling into infidelity. This has created a false issue, one which M. de La Mennais rejects. He has endeavored, and with signal success, to show that there is no discrepancy between religion and liberty; nay, more, that Christianity offers a solid foundation for the broadest freedom, and that, in order to be true to its spirit, its friends must labor with all their might to restore to the people their rights, and to correct all social abuses. He proves that all men are equal before God, and therefore equal one to another. All men have one Father, and are therefore brethren, and ought to treat one another as brothers. This is the Christian law. This law is violated, whenever distinction of races is recognized; whenever one man is clothed with authority over his equals; whenever one man, or a number of men, are invested with certain privileges, which are not shared equally by the whole. As this is the case everywhere, everywhere therefore is the Christian law violated. Everywhere therefore is there suffering, lamentation. The people everywhere groan and travail in pain, sighing to be delivered from their bondage into the glorious liberty of the sons of God. To this deliverance the people have a right. For it every Christian should contend; and they wrong their brethren, deny Christianity, and blaspheme God, who oppose it.

"This is a new doctrine in France. It is something new since the days of the *philosophes,* to undertake to show that Christianity is the religion which favors not kings and privileged orders, but the people, the poor and needy, the wronged and down-trodden. Hitherto the few have made the many submit to the grievous burden under which they groaned, by representing it as irreligious to attempt to remove them. They have enlisted the clergy on their side, and made religion, the very essence of which is justice and love, contribute to the support of oppression. They have deterred the pious from seeking to better their condition, by denouncing all who seek the melioration of society as infidels, but the abbé has put a stop to this unhallowed proceedings. He has nobly vindicated religion and the people. He has turned the tables upon the people's masters, and denounced their masters, not the people, as infidels. He has enlisted religion on the side of freedom; recalled that long-forgotten Gospel, which was glad tidings to the poor, and dared follow the example of Jesus, whom the common people heard gladly, and whom the people's masters crucified between two thieves. He speaks out for freedom, the broadest freedom, not in the tones of the infidel scoffer, but in the name of God, Christ, and man, and with the authority of a prophet. His 'Words of a Believer' has had no parallel since the days of

Jeremiah. It is at once a prophecy, a curse, a hymn, fraught with deep, terrible, and joyful meaning. It is the doom of the tyrant, and the jubilee-shout of the oppressed. We know of no work in which the true spirit of Christianity is more faithfully represented. It proclaims, 'Blessed are the poor, for theirs is the kingdom of heaven;' and woe unto the rich oppressor, the royal spoiler, the Scribes and Pharisees, hypocrites, who bind heavy burdens and lay them on men's shoulders, while they themselves will not move them with one of their fingers."— *The Boston Quarterly Review,* January, 1840, pp. 117-119.

It may not be amiss to place by the side of this bold commendation of the *Words of a Believer,* the judgment pronounced upon that book and its doctrines by the sovereign pontiff, in his encyclical Letter, dated June, 1834, which we find in the Pièces Justificatives, published by M. de La Mennais at the end of his volume entitled, *Affaires de Rome,* Bruxelles, 1837:

"Horruimus sane VV. FF., vel ex primo oculorum obtutu, auctorisque caecitatem miserati intelleximus, quonam scientia prorumpat, quae non secundum Deum sit, sed secundum mundi elementa. Enimvero contra fidem sua illa declaratione solemniter datam, captiosissimis ipse ut plurimum verborum, fictionumque involucris oppugnandam, evertendamque suscepit catholicam doctrinam, quam memoratis nostris literis,* tum de debita erga potestates subjectione, tum de arcenda a populis exitiosa *indifferentismi* con-

---

* *Epistola Encyclica,* August 15, 1832.

tagione, deque frenis injiciendis evaganti opinionum sermonumque licentiae, tum demum de damnanda omnimodo conscientiae libertate, teterrimaque societatum, vel ex cujuscumque falsae religionis cultoribus, in sacrae et publicae rei perniciem conflatarum conspiratione, pro auctoritate humilitati nostrae tradita definivimus.

"Refugit sane animus ea perlegere, quibus ibidem auctor vinculum quodlibet fidelitatis subjectionisque erga principes disrumpere conatur, face undequaque perduellionis immissa qua publici ordinis clades, magistratum contemptus, legum infractio grassetur, omniaque, et sacrae, et civilis potestatis elementa convellantur. Hinc novo et iniquo commento potestatem principum, veluti divinae legi infestam, imo *opus peccati* et *Satanae potestatem* in calumniae portentum traducit, praesidibusque sacrorum easdem, ac imperantibus turpitudinis notas inurit ob criminum molitionumque foedus, quo eos somniat inter se adversus populorum jura conjunctos. Neque tanto hoc ausu contentus omnigenam insuper opinonum, sermonum, conscientiaeque libertatem obtrudit militibusque ad eam *a tyrannide,* ut ait, liberandam dimicaturis fausta omnia ac felicia comprecatur, coetus ac consociationes furiali aestu ex universo qua patet Orbe advocat, et in tam nefaria consilia urgens atque instans compellit, ut eo etiam ex capite monita praescriptaque nostra proculcata abipso sentiamus.

"Piget cuncta hic recensere, quae pessimo hoc impietatis et audaciae foetu ad divina humanque omnia perturbanda congeruntur. Sed illud praesertim indignationem excitat, religionique plane intolerandum est, divinas praescriptiones tantis erroribus adserendis ab auctore afferri, et incautis venditari, eumque ad populos lege obedientiae solvendos, perinde ac si a Deo missus et inspiratus esset, postquam in sacratissimo Trinitatis augustae nomine praefatus est, Sacras Scripturas ubique obtendere, ipsarumque verba quae verba Dei sunt, ad prava hujuscemodi deliramenta inculcanda callide audacterque detorquere, quo fidentius, uti inquiebat S. Bernardus, *pro luce tenebras offundat, et pro melle vel potius in melle venenum propinet, novum cudens populis Evangelium, aliudque ponens fundamentum proeter id quod positum est.*

"Verum tantam hanc sanae doctrinae illatam perniciem silentio dissimulare ab eo vetamur, qui speculatores nos posuit in Israel, ut de errore illos moneamus, quos Auctor et consummator fidei Jesus nostrae curae concredidit.

"Quare autitis nonnullis ex venerabilibus fratribus nostris S. R. E. cardinalibus, motu proprio, et ex certa scientia, deque Apostolicae potestatis plenitudine memoratum l i b r u m, cui titulus: *Paroles d'un Croyant,* quo per impium Verbi Dei abusum populi corrumpuntur ad omnis ordinis publici vincula dissolvenda, ad utramque auctoritatem labefactandam, ad seditiones in imperiis, tumultus, rebellionesque excitandas, fovendas, roborandas, librum ideo propositiones respective falsas, calum niosas, temerarias, inducentes in anarchiam, contrarias Verbo Dei, impias, scandalosas, erroneas jam ab Ecclesia praesertim in Valdensibus, Wiclefitis, Hussitis, aliisque id generis haereticis damnatas continentem, reprobanius, damnamus, ac pro reprobato et damnato in perpetuum haberi volumus, atque decernimus.

"Vestrum nunc erit, venerabiles Fratres, nostris hisce mandatis, quae rei et sacrae et civilis salus et incolumitas, necessario efflagitat, omni contentioni obsecundare, ne scriptum istius modi e latebris ad exitium emissum eo fiat perniciosius, quo magis vesanae novitatis libidini velificatur, et late ut cancer serpit in populis. Muneris vestri sit, urgere sanam de tanto hoc negotio doctrinam, vafritiamque novatorum patefacere, acriusque pro Christiani Gregis custodia vigilare, ut studium religionis, pietas actionum, pax publica floreant et augeantur feliciter. Id sane a vestra fide, et ab impensa vestra pro communi bono instantia fidenter sperimus, ut, eo juvante qui pater est luminum, gratulemur (dicimus cum S. Cypriano) *fuisse intellectum errorem, et retusum, et ideo prostratum, quia agnitum, atque detectum.*"

We hope the judgment of the Holy Father will weigh as much with our readers as that of the editor of *The Boston Quarterly Review.* We had for a time the unenviable honor of being ranked ourselves among those who attempted here and elsewhere to translate Christianity into socialism. There are, perhaps, yet living, persons who remember the zeal and perseverance with which we preached, in the name of the Gospel, the most damnable radicalism.

The general doctrine we asserted was not peculiar to us. We were never remarkable for our originality. We were remarkable, if for any thing, only for the care with which we studied the movement party of our times, seized its great principles, and abandoned ourselves to their direction. We accepted that party, and followed it, with a courage and perseverance worthy of a better cause. The views we put forth were those of our party. They were not peculiar to us then, and they are far less so now. During the last ten or twelve years they have made fearful progress, both at home and abroad. Affecting to be Christian, their advocates invoke the name of Jesus and appeal to the holy Scriptures, the texts of which, with a perverse ingenuity, they accommodate to their socialistic purpose. May Almighty God forgive us the share we had in propagating what we called the *Democracy of Christianity!* We have nothing to palliate our offence or to hide our shame; for, if we knew no better at the time, we might have known better, and our ignorance was culpable. All we can say is, we followed the dominant sentiment of the age, which is a poor excuse for one who professed to be a preacher of the Gospel.

Veiling itself under Christian forms, attempting to distinguish between Christianity and the church, claiming for itself the authority and immense popularity of the Gospel, denouncing Christianity in the name of Christianity, discarding the Bible in the name of the Bible, and defying God in the name of God, socialism conceals from the undiscriminating multitude its true character, and, appealing to the dominant sentiment of the age and to some of our strongest natural inclinations and passions, it asserts itself with terrific power, and rolls on in its career of devastation and death with a force that human beings, in themselves, are impotent to resist. Men are assimilated to it by all the power of their own nature, and by all their reverence for religion. Their very faith and charity are perverted, and their noblest sympathies and their sublimest hopes are made subservient to their basest passions and their most grovelling propensities. Here is the secret of the strength of socialism, and here, is the principal source of its danger.

The open denial of Christianity is not now to be dreaded; the incredulity of the last century is now in bad taste, and can work only under disguise. All the particular heresies which human pride or human perversity could invent are now effete or unfashionable. Every article in the creed has been successively denied, and the work of denial can go no further. The attempt to found a new sect on the denial of any particular article of faith would now only cover its authors with ridicule. The age laughs at Protestantism, and scorns sectarism. The spirit that works in the children of disobedience must, therefore, affect to be Christian, more Christian than Christianity itself, and not only Christian, but *Catholic*. It can manifest itself now, and gain friends, only by acknowledging the church and all Catholic symbols, and substituting for the divine and heavenly sense in which they have hitherto been understood a human and earthly sense. Hence the religious character which socialism attempts to wear. It rejects in name no Catholic symbol; it only rejects the Catholic sense. If it finds fault with the actual church, it is because she is not truly Catholic, does not understand herself, does not comprehend the profound sense of her own doctrines, fails to seize and expound the true Christian idea as it lay in the mind of Jesus, and as this enlightened age is prepared to receive it. The Christian symbol needs a new and a more Catholic interpretation, adapted to our stage in universal progress. Where the old interpretation uses the words God, church, and heaven, you must understand humanity, society, and earth; you will then have the true Christian idea, and bring the Gospel down to the order of nature and within the scope of human reason. But while you put the human and earthly sense upon the old Catholic words, be careful and retain the words themselves. By taking care to do this, you can secure the support of the adherents of Christianity, who, if they meet their old familiar terms, will not miss their old, familiar ideas; and thus you will be able to reconcile the old Catholic world and the new, and to go on with humanity in her triumphant progress through the ages.

Since it professes to be Christian, and really denies the faith, socialism is a heresy; and since by its interpretation it eviscerates the Catholic system of its entire meaning, it is the *résumé* of all the particular heresies which ever have been or can be. The ingenuity of men, aided by the great enemy of souls, can invent no further heresy. All possible heresies are here summed up and actualized in one universal heresy, on which the age is proceeding with all possible haste to erect a counterfeit Catholicity for the reception and worship of Antichrist as soon as he shall appear in person.

"Descend," says La Mennais, "to the bottom of things, and disengage from the wavering thoughts, vain and fleeting opinions, accidentally mingled with it, the powerful principle which, without interruption, ferments in the bosom of society, and what find you but Christianity itself? What is it the people wish, what is it they claim, with a perseverance that never tires, and an ardor that nothing can damp? Is it not the abolition of the reign of force, in order to substitute that of intelligence and rights? Is it not the effective recognition and social realization of equality, inseparable from liberty, the necessary condition and the essential form of which, in the organization of the state, is election, the first basis of the Christian community?

"What, again, do the people wish? What do they demand? The amelioration of the lot of the masses, everywhere so full of suffering; laws for the protection of labor, whence may result a more equitable distribution of the general wealth; that the few shall no longer exercise an exclusive influence for their own profit in the administration of the interests of all; that a legislation which has no bounds, the everlasting refuge of privilege, which it in vain attempts to disguise under lying names, shall no longer, on every side, drive the poor back into their misery; that the goods, destined by the Heavenly Father for all his children, shall become accessible to all; that human fraternity shall cease to be a mockery, and a word without meaning. In short, suscitated by God to pronounce the final judgment upon the old social order, they have summoned it to appear, and recalling the ages which have crumbled away,

they have said to it, 'I was hungry, and ye gave
me not to eat; I was thirsty, and ye gave me not
to drink; I was a stranger, and ye took me not
in; naked, and ye clothed me not; sick and in
prison, and ye did not visit me.' I interrogate you
on the law. Respond. And the old social order is
silent, for it has nothing to answer; and it raises its
hand against the people whom God has appointed
to judge it. But what can it do against the people,
and against God? Its doom is registered on high,
and it will not be able to efface it with the blood
which, for a brief period, it is permitted to shed.

"We cannot, then, but recognize in what is
passing under our eyes the action of *the Christian
principle,* which, having for long ages presided
almost exclusively over individual life, seeks now
to produce itself under a more general and perfect
form, to incarnate itself, so to speak, in social institutions,—the second phase of its development,
of which only the first labor as yet appears.
*Something instinctive and irresistible pushes the
people in this direction.* The few have taken possession of the earth; they have taken possession of
it by wresting from all others even the smallest
part of the common heritage; and the people will
that men live as brothers according to the divine
commandment. They battle for justice and charity; they battle for the doctrine which Jesus Christ
came to preach to the world, and which will save
it in spite of the powers of the world."—*Affaires
de Rome,* pp. 319-321.

This is as artful as it is bold. It wears a pious
aspect, it has divine words on its lips, and almost

unction in its speech. It is not easy for the unlearned to detect its fallacy, and the great body of the people are prepared to receive it as Christian truth. We cannot deny it without seeming to them to be warring against the true interests of society, and also against the Gospel of our Lord. Never was heresy more subtle, more adroit, better fitted for success. How skilfully it flatters the people! It is said, the saints shall judge the world. By the change of a word, the people are transformed into saints, and invested with the saintly character and office. How adroitly, too, it appeals to the people's envy and hatred of their superiors, and to their love of the world, without shocking their orthodoxy or wounding their piety! Surely Satan has here, in socialism, done his best, almost outdone himself, and would, if it were possible, deceive the very elect, so that no flesh should be saved.

What we have said will suffice to show the subtle and dangerous character of socialism, and how, although the majority may recoil from it at present, if logically drawn out by its bolder and more consistent advocates, the age may neverthless be really and thoroughly socialistic. We know that the age seeks with all its energy, as the greatest want of mankind, political and social reforms. Of this there is and can be no doubt. Analyze these reforms and the principles and motives which lead to them, which induce the people in our days to struggle for them, and you will find at the bottom of them all the assumption, that *our good lies in the natural order, and is not attainable by individual effort.* All we see, all we hear, all we read, from whatever quarter it comes, serves to prove that this is the deep and settled conviction of the age. If it were not, these revolutions in France, Italy, Germany, and elsewhere, would have no meaning, no principle, no aim, and would be as insignificant as drunken rows in the streets of our cities.

But the essence of socialism is in this very assumption, that our good lies in the natural order, and is unattainable by individual effort. Socialism bids us follow nature, instead of saying with the Gospel, Resist nature. Placing our good in the natural order, it necessarily restricts it to temporal goods, the only good the order of nature can give. For it, then, evil is to want temporal goods, and good is to possess them. But, in this sense, evil is not remediable or good attainable by individual effort. We depend on nature, which may resist us, and on the conduct of others, which escapes our control. Hence the necessity of social organization, in order to harmonize the interests of all with the interest of each, and to enable each by the union of all to compel nature to yield him up the good she has in store for him. But all men are equal before God, and, since he is just, he is equal in regard to all. Then all have equal rights,—an equal right to exemption from evil, and an equal right to the possession of good. Hence the social organization must be such as to avert equal evil from all, and to secure to each an equal share of temporal goods. Here is socialism in a nut-shell, following as a strictly logical consequence from the principles or assumptions which the age adopts, and on which it everywhere acts. The systems drawn out by Owen, Fourier, Saint-Simon, Cabet, Proudhon, or others, are mere attempts to realize socialism, and may or may not be ridiculous and absurd; but that is nothing to the purpose, if you concede their principle. These men have done the best they could, and you have no right to censure them, as long as you agree with them in principle, unless you propose something better.

Now we agree with La Mennais, that Christianity has a political and social character, and with the editor of *The Boston Quarterly Review,* that Christianity seeks the good of man in this life as well as in the life to come. We say with all our heart, "On the earth was he [our Lord] to found a new order of things, to bring round the blissful ages, and to give to renovated man a foretaste of heaven. It was here the millions were to be blessed with a heaven, as well as hereafter." No doubt of it. But *in* the new order and *by* it,—not out of it and independently of it. Out of the new order and independently of it, the millions are, to say the least, no better off than if it did not exist, and have no right to any portion of its blessings. The socialists, when they attempt to press Christianity into their service, are bad logicians. They are right when they tell us that our Lord came to found a new order of things, for he certainly did come for that purpose; they are right when they tell us that it is Christian to seek a heaven on earth for the millions, for there is a Christian heaven here for all men, if they choose to accept it; but when they say this, they are bound to add that this heaven is in the new order established, and is to be sought in it, and by obedience to its principles. It is Christian to seek that order of happiness which Christianity proposes, by the means which it prescribes; but to seek another order of happiness, and by other means, is not *therefore* necessarily Christian, and may even be antichristian. Here is the point they overlook, and which vitiates all their reasoning.

Let no one say that we allege that man must forego any good while in this world in order to gain heaven hereafter. It would be no great hardship, even if it were so; but our God deals much more liberally with us, and requires us to give up, in order to secure heaven hereafter, only what makes our misery here. The socialist is right in saying that there is good for us even in this world; his error lies in placing that good in the natural order, and in making it unattainable by individual effort. Our good lies not in the natural order, but in the supernatural order,—in that new order which our Lord came to establish. In that order there is all the good we can conceive, and attainable by simple voluntary efforts. Out of that order there is no good attainable either by the efforts of individuals or by association, because out of it there is no good at all. Temporal goods, giving to the term the fullest possible sense, are not good, and, sought for themselves, are productive only of evil. Here is the first error of the socialists. No evil is removable, no good is attainable, as long as any earthly or merely natural end is held to be, for its own sake, a legitimate object of pursuit. There is and can be good for no one, here or hereafter, save in seeking, *exclusively,* the end for which Almighty God has intended us, and by the means and in the way he himself has appointed. Now this end is neither in this world nor of this world, neither in nature nor of nature, and therefore can be gained, can be promoted, by no natural effort, by no natural means,—neither by political changes nor by social changes, neither by political democracy nor by social democracy. These things have and can have no necessary connection with it. It is a mistake, then, to regard them, in themselves, as ever in any degree desirable.

The socialists are right when they say that the Christian law is the law of liberty, but not therefore necessarily right when they term the movements of the people for what they call liberty Christian movements, originating in Christian principle. Undoubtedly, the Christian law is the law of liberty. Our Saviour came to free us from bondage, and whom he makes free is free indeed. In the order he establishes, our highest good, our only good, whether for time or eternity, is entirely independent of the world. Nothing in the universe can hinder us, against our will, from attaining to it. We have only to will it and it is ours, and we are always and everywhere free to will. No one depends on nature or other men for the power to fulfil his destiny,—to gain the end for which he was intended. Here is the Christian doctrine of liberty, the glorious liberty which our religion reveals, and which we know by divine faith is no deception. But the liberty the socialists commend, and which the people are seeking, is not Christian liberty, for it is not liberty at all. Socialism, by its very principle, enslaves us to nature and society, and subjects us to all the fluctuations of time and sense. According to it, man can attain to true good, can gain the end for which he was made, only in a certain political and social order, which it depends on the millions, whom the individual cannot control, to construct, and which, when constructed, may prove to be inconvenient and inadequate, and require to be pulled down and built up again. The individual, it teaches us, can make no advance towards his destiny but in proportion as he secures the cooperation of his race. All men must be brought down or brought up to the same level before he can go to the end for which his God made him; each man's true good is unattainable, till all men are prepared to take "a pull, a strong pull, a long pull, and a pull altogether," to attain theirs! This is slavery, not liberty. Nay, it denies the possibility of liberty, and makes slavery the necessary condition of all men. Is not he a slave who is chained to nature for his good, or to a social organization which does not exist, and which depends on the wisdom, the folly, the passions or instincts, the whims or caprices of other men to create or to destroy? Who can deny it? He only is free, he only knows what freedom is, who tramples the world beneath his feet, who is independent of all the accidents of time and space, of all created beings, and who has but to will and all heaven is his, and remains his, though the entire universe fall in ruins around him.

Undoubtedly Christianity requires us to remove all evil, and in seeking to remove evil we follow the Christian principle; but what the socialists call evil, and the people in revolt are seeking to remove, is not evil. Nothing is evil but that which turns a man away from his end, or interposes a barrier to his advance towards it. Nothing but one's own sin can seize the brand and turn on the tyrant, and DIE shall he or we. It is an awful thing to see brother hewing and hacking the flesh of brother, and strewing the ground with the limbs and trunks of precious human beings; but it is more awful to see a whole nation of workingmen bound hand and foot, dying starved, while there is bread enough and to spare; a thousand times more awful in time of peace and plenty, to see poor human mothers driven to devour the flesh of their own offspring, of the dear ones who have drawn life from their own breasts!

But we must pass not too lightly over this subject. Can there be a more sorrowful sight, can there be a stronger condemnation of an order of things, than this simple fact of men, able-bodied men, with rational souls and cunning right hands, willing, begging to work, and yet finding no work to do whereby they can get their victuals? Certainly not, say all men with one voice. Well, then, friends and countrymen, is it only in England that we stumble on this fact? What, we ask, are we coming to in this country, here where there are so many millions of acres of rich, fertile lands, waiting to be tilled? We have not yet come, it may be, to the Glasgow lanes and Stockport cellars, of which Carlyle speaks, but we *have* come very near to the St. Ives workhouses; but we have come to the point where there are many thousands of our people who can keep the life in them only as fed by the grudging hand of public or private charity. In 1829, it was reckoned that in Boston, New York, Philadelphia and Baltimore, there were eighteen thousand females, sempstresses mostly, unable to obtain work for more than two-thirds of the

time; and yet if getting work all the time, for sixteen
hours a day, receiving therefor only about sixteen
dollars a year with which to furnish fuel, food and
clothing; many of these wives with sick and disabled
husbands; many of them widows with two, three and
four small children to support. So said the benevolent Matthew Carey. The matter must be worse now.
In this wealthy, charitable, industrious, Christian city
of Boston, where we now write, we have come, the
last winter, to our bread and soup societies! Bread
and soup societies for the poor, already in this
blessed land of America, free, democratic America,
and in the very heart of thrifty, religious New England! So alas! have we managed it. We may wince
at the statement; may offer all manner of explanations of it, such as influx of foreigners, stagnation of
trade, want of confidence, John Tyler administrations; but there stands the fact, in open, broad daylight, that able-bodied men and women, ready and
willing to work for their food, nay, coming to you,
and with tears in their eyes, begging you to give them
work, have been kept through the long winter just
above the starving point,—and we fear in all cases
not above,—only by soup and bread dealt out by
charitable societies in tin porringers. Just before the
breaking out of the French revolution, some poor
peasants came to the court, and asked for bread and
got—a new gallows; which shows how it fares with
the people under the monarchical method of governing. St. Ives work-houses, Glasgow lanes, Stockport
cellars, and the present condition of Ireland, where,
out of a population of eight millions, one-third are
reduced to feed on third-rate potatoes, these scantily

obtained, and failing altogether for nearly a third of the year, show how they manage matters under an aristocracy. Soup and bread societies for men and women able and willing to work, in Boston and other cities, show to what a pass things may come under the virtuous and intelligent rule of the democracy; which, considering the advantages with which we started, the vast quantities of fertile lands still lying waste, and our youth, vigor, and elasticity, is pretty well, and may be thought to prove that, if we have not as yet come up with kings and nobilities, we are in a fair way of overtaking them, and, if it were possible, of even going beyond them.

Here we are, then, in our own country, in the most favored part of it, renowned the world over for its industry, and thrift, frugality and economy, and wise management, come to such a pass that a portion —we will hope as yet not a large portion—of our population can get no work, no opportunity whereby to eat their bread in the sweat of their face. The fact is undeniable. It cannot be glossed over. It is here. We can lay our hands on it. These soup and bread societies are no fiction. Alas! the necessity there was that they should be, is also no fiction. With our own eyes we have seen poor children gliding along the cold streets, thinly clad, with their tin cans to receive their modicum. We have set our own feet in the miserable dwellings of those who have been thus fed, and knelt down in prayer by the poor man dying of a fever brought on by anxiety and insufficient food.

The newspapers told us some time since of a well educated, respectable man, brought up before our police for stealing a parcel from a dry goods shop.

On the trial, it came out that he was well nigh starved, could get no work, and had taken the desperate resolution of stealing in order to gain the *privilege* of being sent to the *House of Correction* so as not to die starved. To such straits had it come with him, that he regarded it as a favor to be sent to the House of Correction. A poor man, a worthy mechanic, in Philadelphia, this last winter, can find no work; comes to the magistrate and begs to be locked up in the cell of the City Prison; so that he may find the food which he knows no other method of procuring. One rejoices to know that the benevolent magistrate granted him his request.

Now, in all soberness, we ask, if a state of things in which such incidents can occur, do occur, however rare, is the best that we can have in this nineteenth century, in this blessed land of America, of universal suffrage, universal education, under the blessed light of the Gospel, dotted all over with industrial establishments, school-houses, and churches? Is this a God's world, or is it a devil's world? O, dear countrymen, say what you will, decidedly this is not a question for England only; it is also a question for you. In God's name, in humanity's name, do not blink this question. Answer us, nay, not us, but your own hearts, if you are prepared, in the face of that sun which shines so gloriously on all, the lowly thatched cottage as well as on the lordly palace, to say that you solemnly believe that in the decrees of Providence, in the richest of infinite Love, and of infinite Grace, there was nothing better for us than these bread and soup societies, this begging to be locked up in jail, and stealing in order to be sent to the House of Correction, so that the life may be left in us?

We might go further, in proof of the sad state to which we are coming or have already come. We are told, on tolerable authority, that in this city of Boston, which we take it is the model city of this country, there are some four thousand wretched prostitutes out of a population of about one hundred thousand. This fact is not only a lucid commentary on our morals, but also on the difficulty there is in getting a living by honest industry; since prostitution is resorted to in this and all other countries rarely through licentiousness, but chiefly, almost wholly, through poverty. We are also told by the agents of the police, who have the best means of knowing, that the principal supply of these victims to poverty and men's infamy, comes from the factories in the neighboring towns!—no uninteresting comment on the workings of the factory system, built up by our banks and high tariffs, and which the chiefs of our industry have taken, and are taking so much pains to fasten on the country!

But whence come these sad results? There must be somewhere a fatal vice in our social and industrial arrangements, or there would not, could not, be these evils to complain of. Never, till within these last few centuries, were men, able and willing to work, brought to the starving point in times of peace, and in the midst of plenty. "Gurth," says Carlyle, "born thrall of Cedric the Saxon, tended pigs in the wood, and did get some parings of the pork. The four-footed worker has already *got* all that the two-handed one is clamoring for. There is not a horse in all England, able and willing to work, but *has* due food and lodging; and goes about sleek-coated, satisfied in heart. Is this such a platitude of a world, that all working horses shall be well fed, and innumerable working men and women die starved?" We do not believe it; we will, thank Heaven! believe no such thing. Whence, where, and what, then, is the fundamental vice of our modern society, especially in this our Saxon portion of it?

On this question Mr. Carlyle's book throws some light, though, it must be owned, often of the fitful and uncertain sort. In general, and in rather vague terms, it may be answered that this vice is in the fact that men have substituted the worship of Mammon for the worship of God. Mammonism has become the religion of Saxondom, and God is not in all our thoughts. We have lost our faith in the noble, the beautiful, the just; we have lost our faith in the Highest, and have come to believe in and to worship the lowest, even Mammon,—

"Mammon, the least erected spirit that fell
From heaven; for even in heaven his looks and
    thoughts
Were always downward bent, admiring more
The riches of heaven's pavement, trodden gold,
Than aught divine or holy else enjoy'd
In beatific vision."

The demonstration of this fact, and a full and impartial description of the worship of Mammon, would be a service of no mean worth to our countrymen; but who shall undertake to perform it? The other day we chanced to drop a word which was misconstrued into a growing distrust of liberty, and voices in all parts of the country were loud and harsh in condemnation; should we now but *exercise* the liberty of telling our countrymen the simple truth, and of directing their attention to the error, the original sin whence has sprung the present disordered state of society, there would be no end to the berating we should receive from these same loud and harsh voices,—ready always to cry lustily for liberty, but most ready to condemn all who are really her efficient friends and servants. We boast, in this blessed land of Washington and Jefferson, of our freedom; we are free, ay, free as the winds that drive through our valleys or sweep over our broad plains and inland oceans,—to echo the public voice, to have no opinion of our own, and to say only what everybody believes or nobody takes the trouble to disbelieve. We knew, once upon a time, a young man, brought up in the wild freedom lingering yet in some few of our mountain homes; an earnest, simple spirit, who had the strange fancy when he came to dwell in cities and in the midst of civilization, that he should be sincere, transparent, and speak out always, when speaking at all, the simple, naked truth, without any circumlocution or reticence, as he found himself commanded by the Highest, and as all public Teachers and Able Editors exhorted him and all men to do. Foolish youth from the mountains! It was never intended by these Lights of their age, that thou shouldst *exercise* freedom of thought and freedom of speech, but merely that thou shouldst, in high-sounding and well-turned periods, laud freedom of thought and freedom of speech, and tell thy admiring countrymen what fine things, beautiful things they are. Poor young man! We own that, with all thy folly, we loved thee. Thou hadst a noble heart, a brave spirit, and we confess that we have watered with our tears the turf on thy early grave. But notwithstanding our inward admiration of thy free and generous nature, we have finally resolved to take warning by thy melancholy fate, and to be like our countrymen generally,—wise and prudent. Humbly do we beg pardon for having said in our folly, that what the demagogues tell them about their intelligence and virtue is all a humbug. It was an unwise, an imprudent word. We will no more repeat it. We will henceforth be silent, merely pointing, in our good city of Boston, to soup and bread societies for able-bodied men and women, ready, willing, begging to work, who yet can get no work to do; to four thousand victims of man's infamy, the number kept good by a surplus factory population; to the honest, intelligent, even well-educated man, driven to steal, in order to gain the, to him, inestimable favor of being sent to the House of Correction. Dear friends, most wise and virtuous demagogues, all you say of the dear people, of their intelligence and virtue, is, no doubt, very true, very sweet—for you have sweet breaths—and may we never be again left to question your veracity; but these four thousand . . . , these soup and bread societies, this privilege of being sent to the House of Correction, or of being locked up in a dungeon?

We have some thoughts on the origin of the evils we have touched upon, but which, were we to tell them all plainly, and honestly, and unreservedly, would, we fear, create such a hubbub and general confusion, that we should lose henceforth the power not only to be heard, but even to speak at all. There can be no question that within the last three hundred years there has been a most wonderful increase of industrial activity; of man's productive power; and of the aggregate wealth of the world. Great industries, so to speak, have within these three hundred years sprung up, never before conceived of; man has literally made the winds his messengers, and flames of fire his ministers; all nature works for him; the mountains sink, and the valleys rise before him; the land and the ocean fling out their treasures to him; and time and space are annihilated by his science and skill. All this is unquestionable. On the other hand, equally unquestionable is it to him who has looked on the matter with clear vision, that in no three hundred years known to us, since men began to be born and to die on this planet, upon the whole, it has fared worse, for soul or for body, with the great mass of the laboring population. Our advance, it would seem, has been that ordered by the militia captain, an "advance backwards!" This statement may or may not make sad work with our theories of progress of the race, progress of light, of political and social well-being, and all that: but it is a fact, an undeniable, a most mournful fact, which get over we cannot, try we never so hard.

For these last three hundred years we have lost or been losing our faith in God, in heaven, in love, in justice, in eternity, and been acquiring faith only in human philosophies, in mere theories concerning supply and demand, wealth of nations, self-support-ing, labor-saving governments; needing no virtue, wisdom, love, sacrifice, or heroism on the part of their managers; working out for us a new Eden, converting all the earth into an Eldorado land, and enabling us all to live in Eden Regained. We have left behind us the living faith of the earlier ages; we have abandoned our old notions of heaven and hell; and have come, as Carlyle well has it, to place our heaven in success in money matters, and to find the infinite terror which men call hell, only in not succeeding in making money. We have thus come—where we are. Here is a fact worth meditating.

We boast of our light; we denounce old feudalism and the middle ages, and fancy it worth a *Te Deum* that we have got rid of them; and yet, the impartial and clear-sighted historian being asked, what period he lingers on, when, all things considered, it proved best with the great mass of the European population, answers, without hesitation, the period when feudalism and the church were in their greatest glory; that is, from the tenth to the end of the fourteenth century. Compare the condition of what Carlyle calls the "workers" of England, the land of our ancestors, during that period, with the condition of the corresponding class at present, and one is almost struck dumb by the contrast. Cotton, as Carlyle says, is cheaper, but it is harder to get a shirt to one's back. Cotton is produced at two pence an ell, and shirts lie piled up in warehouses, and men go about with bare backs. For food, even Gurth born thrall of Cedric, did get some parings of the pork; the poor mother and father of the Stockport cellar, alas! none. For spiritual food, the poorest had faith and were instructed at least in the elements of the Christian religion; inquiries recently made into the condition of the population employed in the English collieries, show that human beings do grow up in the nineteenth century, in rich, ay, and *Christian* England, who know not even the name of their Maker, save by hearing it desecrated; and all accounts agree that the morals of the colliers are superior to the morals of the factory operatives. In the highest departments of thought and genius, the contrast is hardly less striking; our most advanced philosophers were anticipated; we are scarcely able even to copy the Gothic church, the last word of Christian architecture; and Dante has in poetry no rival, unless it be Shakspeare.

During these and the preceding four hundred years, more work was done for humanity, under an intellectual and social point of view, than was ever done, in a like period, since history began. A writer, not to be suspected of undue partiality, in touching upon this period and upon the action of the church, is forced to say, "During the greater part of that period, by means of her superior intelligence and virtue, she—the church—ruled the state, modified its actions, and compelled its administrators to consult the rights of man, by protecting the poor, the feeble, and the defenceless. It is not easy to estimate the astonishing progress she effected for civilization during that long period called by narrow-minded and bigoted Protestant historians, the dark ages. Never before had such labors been performed for humanity. Never before had there been such an immense body, as the Christian clergy, animated by a common spirit, and directed by a common will and intelligence to the culture of the moral virtues and the arts of peace. Then was tamed the wild barbarian, and the savage heart made to yield to the humanizing influences of tenderness, gentleness, meekness, humility, and love; then imperial crown and royal sceptre paled before the crosier; and the representative of him who lived, and toiled, and preached, and suffered, and died in obscurity, in poverty and disgrace, was exalted and made himself felt in the palace and in the cottage, in the court and in the camp, striking terror into the rich and noble, and pouring the oil and wine of consolation into the bruised heart of the poor and friendless. Wrong, wrong have they been, who have complained that kings and emperors were subjected to the spiritual head of Christendom. It was well for man that there was a power above the brutal tyrants called emperors, kings, and barons, who rode rough-shod over the humble peasant and artisan,—well that there was a power, even on earth, that could touch their cold and atheistic hearts, and make them tremble as the veriest slave. The heart of humanity leaps with joy, when a murderous Henry is scourged at the tomb of Thomas à Becket, or when another Henry waits barefoot, shivering with cold and hunger, for days, at the door of the Vatican, or when a Pope grinds his foot into the neck of a prostrate Frederick Barbarossa. Aristocratic Protestantism, which has never dared enforce its discipline on royalty and nobility, may weep over the exercise of such power, but it is to the existence and exercise of that power that the *People* owe *their* existence, and the doctrine of man's equality with man, its progress."*

The writer here quoted, is hardly just to the feudal aristocracy. The old feudal lords and barons were not a mere dilettante aristocracy, a mere unworking aristocracy, consuming without doing aught for the general work of production. They were, in fact, then a working aristocracy, and did work in their rude way, and contrived to do no little work of the governing sort; for which the governed did fare the better. In matters of fighting they did the hardest, and bore the first and heaviest blows. It was their special right, not to lead only, but to do the work of killing and of being killed. They did in some sense, in return for what they received, yield a protection to the people, and take some kind of care of them. If the serf, before serfage was abolished, labored for his lord, the lord owed him a reciprocal obligation, and must see that he had wherewithal to eat and to be clothed. If fixed to the soil, the serf had a right to his support from it. These old barons, moreover, did not entirely neglect the commons in contending for the interest of their own order, as we may learn by consulting Magna Charta. The service they rendered to society, was no doubt an inadequate return for what they received; but nevertheless it was some return, and the castle of the Lord, *law-ward,* according to Carlyle, was a tower of strength not only to its owner, but also to the hamlet lying under its walls; and the proud dame, my Lady, *Loaf-distributor,* was not seldom a gentle benefactress to the humble, confiding, and grateful peasants. If it was a privilege to

* Ante. p. 67.

be high-born, so was it a privilege to have the high-born among us.

On this part of the subject, Mr. Carlyle's book may be consulted with considerable advantage. He has not said all he might, nor all that we wish he had. He has given us a very pleasant glimpse of one aspect of life in the middle ages, that represented by the Ancient Monk; but we wish it had comported with his plan to have given us a clearer insight into the condition of the rural population, the cultivators of the soil, the thralls, sockmen, farmers, peasants, and their relation to their landlords, masters, or owners. We confess that on this subject we are not so well informed as we would be. It is a great and interesting subject, but from the glimpses we catch now and then of it, we are fully convinced that the relation between the two classes which then subsisted, was decidedly preferable to that which now is; even your modern slaveholder is obliged to recognize a relation between him and his slave of a more generous and touching nature than any recognized by the master-worker between himself and his workman. The slave when old or sick must be protected, provided for, whether the owner receives any profit from him or not; the master-worker has discharged all the obligation to his operative he acknowledges when he has paid him the stipulated wages. These wages may be insufficient for mere human subsistence, and the poor worker must die; but what is that to the master-worker? Has he not paid all he agreed to pay, even to the last farthing, promptly? We have not heard on our southern plantations, of Stockport cellars, of bread and soup societies by the charitable, and men stealing in order to be sent to the House of Correction so as not to starve. This much we can say of the slave, that if he will tend pigs in the wood, he shall have some parings of the pork, and so long as his master has full barns he is not likely to starve; would we could say as much of the hired laborer always!

But the chief thing we admire in the middle ages, is that men did then believe in God, they did believe in some kind of justice, and admit that man, in order to reap, must in some way aid the sowing; that man did, whatever his condition, owe some kind of duty to his fellow man; and admit it, not merely in theory, in caucus speeches, or in loud windy professions, but seriously in his heart and his practice. But we have changed all that, we have called the religion of the middle ages superstition, the philosophy which then was cultivated, miserable jargon, and the governing which then went on, tyranny and oppression. We have learned to blush at the page of history which speaks of Hildebrand, and St. Anselm, and the enfranchisement of the communes, and would if we could blot it out. It is a reproach to a man in these times and in this country to name it without execrating it. The age which covered Europe over with its Gothic churches, and with foundations and hospitals for the poor, produced St. Anselm, Abelard, St. Bernard, and Dante, Chaucer, old John of Gaunt, and Magna Charta, De Montfort, William Longbeard, Philip Van Arteveld, Roger Bacon, Albert Magnus, John of Fidanza, Duns Scotus, and St. Thomas Aquinas, is a blank in human history! Thank God we have outgrown it, got rid of it. We are no longer superstitious; we have made away with the old monks whose maxim was "work is worship;" we have struck down the last of the barons; we are free; we have the Gospel of the cotton mill, *laissez-faire,* save who can, and the devil take the hindmost, and we can do what we please with our own. A notable change this, and worth considering. How was it brought about, and what has been the gain?

We cannot go fully into the inquiry this question opens up. The middle ages brought the human race forward not a little. What most strikes us is the moral and spiritual exaltation which everywhere meets us. Man, through the faith nurtured and strengthened in him by the church, became great, noble, chivalrous, energetic. This immense spiritual force accumulated in the interior of man during the four centuries named, overflows in the activity, bold adventure, vast enterprises, and important discoveries which commence in the fifteenth century. We note here four things resulting from it, which have especially contributed to the change of which we speak: the invention or rather general use of gunpowder; the revival of letters; the invention of printing; and the maritime discoveries in the East and the West. These are considered, we believe, the principal agents in effecting what we have been pleased to call the progress of modern society.

1. The art of war, as carried on prior to the introduction of fire-arms, which did not come into general use before the fifteenth century, was accessible for the most part only to the noble class and their retainers. It required so long a training, so great bodily strength and dexterity, and so much outlay in the

equipments of the individual warrior, that artisans and peasants could make up but a small part, and never a very efficient part of an army. The chief reliance was, and necessarily, upon the nobility, the knights, and gentlemen. In this case the king was always more or less dependent on his nobles, and could rarely go to war without their assent and active aid. This restrained the royal power, and prevented the *centralization* of power in the hands of the monarch. The invention and general use of fire-arms lessened the importance of the cavalry, in which only the lords and gentlemen served, and increased that of the infantry, composed of commoners. The monarch was able to dispense then, to a certain extent, with the services of his nobility, and to find his support in the people, artisans and peasants, easily collected and speedily disciplined. By thus introducing the infantry into the royal armies, as the main reliable branch of the service, a rude shock was given to the power and independence of the nobles. From that moment the feudal nobility began to wane, and the power and independence of the monarch to increase.

The decrease of the power of the nobility served to weaken that of the church. The people naturally, with their instinctive wisdom, would cleave to the monarch, who employed them in his armies. They saw themselves now admitted to a share in an employment which had been previously, for the most part, the prerogative of their masters, and proud of being admitted to the high privilege of killing and being killed, they fancied that they were by this admission virtually enfranchised, and raised to an equality with those who had hitherto been their superiors. The rudest peasant, with a firelock in this hand, was more than a match for the bravest, strongest, best diciplined, and completely armed knight. Hence, all the tendencies of the people would be, in any contest, so far as possible, to support their royal masters. In the commons, then, royalty found its support against the nobility, and even against the church. At least, by admitting the common people into the royal armies, royalty weakened, or to some extent neutralized their affection for the ecclesiastical power, which in any contest between it and the church was of vast importance.

2. The revival of letters, as it is called, that is, of the study and reverence of *heathen* literature, which followed the taking of Constantinople by the Turks, had also a powerful influence in bringing about the change we have noted. The church, during the middle ages, had paid great attention to education; it had covered Europe over with universities and schools. In the early part of the fifteenth century, education was almost as general throughout the principal states of Europe as it is now; the actual amount of instruction one is tempted to believe was greater, though perhaps a smaller number could read and write. The Bible had been translated into the vernacular language of Englishmen prior even to Wyckliffe, which would indicate that the Saxon population were able to read. There was, at any rate, a very general mental activity throughout Europe, as the relics of the popular ballads and literature of the time bear witness. The mind was prepared for the new literature which was then brought to light. The

Greek scholars, with Greek subtlety and Greek sophistry, were dispersed, by the taking of Constantinople, over the principal Latin States; the study of the ancient heathen literature went with them, and the several schools of ancient Greek philosophy had their disciples and champions in the very bosom and among the high dignitaries of the church herself. Its obvious and unquestionable superiority, as to the perfection and beauty of its form, over the richer, profounder, more varied, and earnest, but less polished literature of the fathers and the church, secured it a ready adoption and an almost universal authority. In this fact we are to discover a powerful cause operating to destroy the power of the church and the order of civilization it had built up.

During the preceding centuries the nobles, being almost wholly occupied with governing, fighting, and doing their part, as they could, in the general affairs of society, had left literature almost entirely to the church. But, in the fifteenth century, in consequence of the change already noted in the art of war, their original occupation was to a considerable extent taken away, and they began to turn their attention towards letters. The schools and universities began to send out scholars from the lay commoners, and we had for the first time in Europe, since the establishment of the barbarians, an educated and literary laity. The surface of education had been greatly extended; and alway in proportion as education extends laterally does it lose in depth. The diffusion of education among the laity had created an immense class of superficial thinkers, half-educated, always worse, more to be dreaded than those who have no education, as simplicity is always preferable to ignorance fancying itself wisdom. We had then just the state of mind necessary to welcome the heathen literature of which we speak. Its very superficialness, want of earnestness and strength, when compared with Christian literature, was recommendation, and facilitated its reception.

The effect of this revived heathen literature, on the tone of thought, and its general bearings on Christian faith, are not always duly considered. The fathers of the church in the first five centuries had culled out from it all that Christianity would assimilate to itself, and made it an integral part of the common literary and philosophic life of the church. We had in the church all of heathen Greece and Rome that was worth retaining, or that could be retained in consistency with our faith as Christians. The human race then did not need the revival. No good could come of it; for nothing new, but exploded heathenism, was to be obtained from it. The revival was then in very deed a revival of heathenism. It was hostile to Christianity, and deeply prejudicial to the faith of Christians. And so history has proved it. We speak advisedly. We know very well the estimation in which the ancient classics are held, and that one may as well speak against the Bible as against them. But, what is this so much boasted classical literature? We admit the exquisiteness of its form; the perfection of the execution; we, too, have our admiration for the divine Plato; we love as well as others an Aristotle, and find much in the Greek tragedians that we love and admire; but we cannot forget that the whole body of ancient Greek and

Roman literature is heathenish, wanting in true religious conception, in genuine love of man, in true, deep, living, Christian piety. Permit us to quote here, what we wrote on this subject some seven years ago, from another point of view, it is true, and with a far different aim, but still with substantially the same faith:

"By means of the classics, the scholars of the fifteenth century were introduced to a world altogether unlike, and much *superior* [perhaps not] to that in which they lived,—to an order of ideas wholly diverse from those avowed or tolerated by the church. They were enchanted. They had found the ideal of their dreams. They became disgusted with the present, they repelled the civilization effected by the church, looked with contempt on its fathers, saints, martyrs, schoolmen, troubadours, knights, and ministrels, and sighed and yearned, and labored to reproduce Athens or Rome.

"And what was that Athens and that Rome which seemed to them to realize the very ideal of the perfect? We know very well today what they were. They were material; through the whole period of their historical existence, it is well known that the material or temporal order predominated over the spiritual. * * * Human interests, the interests of mankind in time and space predominate. Man is the most conspicuous figure in the group. He is everywhere, and his imprint is upon everything. Industry flourishes; commerce is encouraged; the state is constituted and tends to democracy; citizens assemble to discuss their common interests; the orator harangues them; the aspirant courts them; the warrior and the statesman render them an account of their doings, and await their award. The *People*—not the gods—will, decree, make, unmake, or modify the laws. Divinity does not become incarnate, as in the Asiatic world; but men are deified. History is not theogony, but a record of human events and transactions. Poetry sings heroes, the great and renowned of earth, or chants at the festal board and at the couch of voluptuousness. Art models its creations after human forms, for human pleasure, or human convenience.

"There are gods and temples, and priests and oracles, and augurs and auguries, but they are not like those we meet where spiritualism reigns. The gods are all anthropomorphous. Their forms are the perfection of the human. The allegorical beasts, the strange beasts, compounded of parts of many known and unknown beasts, which meet us in Indian, Egyptian, and Persian mythology, as symbols of the gods, are extinct. Priests are not a caste, as under spiritualism, springing from the head of Brahma, and claiming superior sanctity and power as their birthright; but simple police officers. Religion is merely a function of the state. * * * Numa introduces or organizes polytheism at Rome, for the purpose of governing the people by means of appeals to their sentiment of the holy; and the Roman pontifex maximus was never more than a master of police.

"In classical antiquity religion is a function of the state. It is the same under Protestantism.

Henry VIII, of England, declares himself supreme head of the church, not by virtue of his
spiritual character, but by virtue of his character
as a temporal prince. The Protestant princes of
Germany are *protectors* of the church; and all
over Europe there is an implied contract between
the state and the ecclesiastical authorities. The
state pledges itself to support the church, on
condition that the church support the state. Ask
the kings, nobility, or even church dignitaries, why
they support religion, and they will answer with
one voice, 'Because the people cannot be kept in
order, cannot be made to submit to their rulers,
and because civil society cannot exist, without it.'
The same, or a similar answer will be returned by
almost every political man in this country: and
truly may it be said, that religion is valued by
the Protestant world as an auxiliary to the state,
as a mere matter of police.

"Under the reign of spiritualism all questions
are decided by authority. The church commanded,
and men were to obey, or be counted rebels
against God. Materialism, by raising up man and
the state, makes the reason of man, or the reason
of the state paramount to the commands of the
church. Under Protestantism, the state in most
cases, the individual reason in a few, imposes
the creed on the church. The king and parliament
of Great Britain determine the faith the clergy
must profess and maintain; the Protestant princes
in Germany have the supreme control of the
symbols of the church, the right to enact what
creed they please."*

---

* Ante, pp. 17-20.

The revival and general study of the classics, tended by their character to destroy the power of the church of the middle ages, to introduce an order of thought favorable to the supremacy of the civil over the ecclesiastical order, the effect of which is seen in the sudden growth of the monarchical or royal authority, which took place at the close of the fifteenth century, and the beginning of the sixteenth. The influence of this heathen literature, breaking the authority of the church, and the use of fire-arms superseding to some extent the co-operation of the old feudal nobility, combining, enabled the European potentates to shake off the authority of the church, and to establish themselves in their independence. The cause of Protestantism was eminently the cause of the kings, and under the social and political aspect,—the only aspect in which we now consider, or wish to consider the subject at all, —was the cause of the people, only so far as it was for their advantage, to lose the protection of the church, and the feudal noble, and to come under the unrestrained authority of the civil magistrate,— an authority which was not slow to degenerate into unbearable tyranny, as we see in the English revolution in the seventeenth century, and the French in the eighteenth. But fire-arms and classical literature succeeded, by bringing the laity into the literary class, and the commoners into the armies, in breaking down the authority of the church, destroying the old feudal nobility, and in establishing the independence of kings and the temporal governments, and not merely in what were called Protestant countries; for the principle of Protestantism triumphed throughout Europe for a season, in the countries remaining Catholic in name, as well as in those that became avowedly Protestant. Francis I and Charles V would have done what did Henry VIII, the princes of the north of Germany, and Gustavus Adolphus, if they had not humbled the church, and for a time compelled the Holy See to succumb to their interests and wishes.

The independence of civil governments established, and the kings, freed from the dominion of the church and the checks of the old feudal barons, were not slow to adopt a purely worldly policy; and before the close of the fifteenth century, the policy now termed Machiavellian, was adopted and avowed by every court in Europe,—that is to say, a policy wholly detached from all moral and religious doctrines or principles. Machiavelli was born at Florence, of a noble family, in 1469, and, though often execrated, was a great and learned man, and by no means ignorant or destitute of morality. He was *the politician,* the statesman of his epoch, and may be consulted as the highest authority for the maxims on which rested the policy of the European courts at the period under consideration.

3. The invention of printing on movable types, we are far from thinking,—far, very far from wishing to intimate,—is not destined to effect the greatest good; but we are equally decided that, up to the present moment, it would be difficult to say whether it has been productive of the more good or evil. We will not so far dishonor ourselves as even to say that we are the friends of knowledge and universal enlightenment; we know no advocates of ignorance;

we have no sympathy with those, if such there be, who would withhold education from any portion of the human race; but we repeat that we regard half-education as worse than no education. We are not ashamed to avow our agreement with Pope, that

"A little learning is a dangerous thing
Drink deep, or taste not the Pierian spring;
There shallow draughts intoxicate the brain,
But drinking deeply sobers us again."

The great mass of our American people can read and do read the newspapers, and many other things; and all of them fancy themselves competent to sit in judgment on all matters human and divine. They are equal to the profoundest philosophical speculations, the loftiest theological dogmas, and the abstrusest political problems. Filled with a sense of their own wisdom and capacity for sound judgment, they lose all teachableness, and are really in a more deplorable state than if they made no pretensions to general intelligence. Unquestionably we must pass through this stage of superficial knowledge, which merely engenders pride, conceit self-will, before we can come to that of true enlightenment; and therefore we do not complain, but submit to the present evil, consoling ourselves with the hope of the glory hereafter to be revealed. Nevertheless, it is an evil, deny it who will.

Printing, by multiplying books and making the great mass of the people readers, serves to foster the spirit of individualism, which is only one form of supreme selfishness. He who has not the humility to learn, the meekness to obey, who feels that he has no superior, but that he is as good as you, will soon come to feel that he owes no duty but to himself; and that the true morality in his case is to take care of Number One. In this way the invention of printing, co-operating with the causes already mentioned, tended to destroy the church and nobility of the middle ages, to substitute pride, intractableness and egotism for the old spirit of submission and self-denial, and therefore aided on the change we have noted. Ignorance and self-sufficiency pervert Heaven's choicest blessings; and the Bible itself, thrown into the hands of the mass incompetent to its interpretation or right understanding, become, we are often obliged to own, a savor of death unto death, and generates endless sects and interminable strife, as fatal to the cause of piety as to individual and public happiness.

4. On the heels of all this, materialism in philosophy, virtually if not expressly, arrogant individualism in matters of faith, selfishness or a refined or even gross Epicureanism in morals, and the independence and centralization of the civil power in the hands of the absolute monarch, adopting and acting, as Caesar Borgia and Ferdinand of Aragon, on a policy wholly detached from religion and morality, came the discovery of the passage round the Cape of Good Hope, and of this Western Continent. Already had men's minds been drawn off from high spiritual subjects; already had they begun to be heathenized, and of the earth earthy; the church was reduced to be a tool of the state; the minister of religion shorn of his sacred authority and converted into a police officer. The world was ripe for a new order of things; for entering into the career of industrial aggrandizement, the

accumulation of treasures on earth, forgetful that moth and rust may corrupt and thieves break through and steal. The newly discovered worlds afforded the means both of increasing and of satisfying this tendency. A sudden change came over the whole industrial world; visions of untold wealth floated before all eyes; and men who would in the twelfth century have been content to lead lives of self-denial, and to labor as peaceful monks, seeking in their quiet retreats for the crown of God's approval, were crossing all oceans, penetrating into all forests, digging into all mountains, in pursuit of GOLD. The love of gold supplanted the love of God; and the professed followers of Christ no longer made pilgrimages to the Holy Land, but to the Gold Coast, to Florida, Mexico, and Peru, in pursuit not of the sacred relics of saints and martyrs, monuments consecrated by faith and love, but of the fabled Eldorado. Commerce took a new flight, and in a few years manufactures began to flourish, great industrial establishments to spring up; science and inventive genius came in— Manchester, Leeds, Lowell,—an immense operative population wanting shirts to their backs while shirts are lying idle, piled up in warehouses, and they starving in the midst of abundance!

We have here glanced at some of the causes which have operated to destroy the religious faith of the middle ages, to abolish the worship of God in Christian lands, and to introduce the worship of Mammon, —all-triumphant Mammon. Going along through the streets of Boston the other day, we remarked that it has become the fashion to convert the basement floors of our churches into retail shops of various kinds of merchandise. How significant! The church is made to rest on TRADE; Christ on Mammon. Was any thing ever more typical? The rents of these shops in some cases, we are told, pay the whole expense of the minister's salary. Poor minister! if thou shouldst but take it into thy head to rebuke Mammon, as thy duty bids thee, and to point out the selfishness and iniquity of the dominant spirit of trade, thy underpinning would slide from under thee, and thou wouldst- - - - . But land is valuable; and why should it lie idle all days in the week but one, because a meeting-house stands on it? Ay, sure enough. O, blessed thrift, great art thou, and hast learned to coin thy God and to put him out at usury! But what hast thou gained? Thou are care-worn and haggard, and with all thy economies, begrudging Heaven the small plat of ground for his temple,— Heaven who gives thee all, this whole earth, so much broader than thou canst cultivate, thou hast to provide bread and soup societies for the poor starving men and women, who would work, but can get no work.

Here we are, in Ireland, every third person reduced to live on third-rate potatoes, these scantily obtained, and for only thirty-six weeks in the year; in England and Scotland, with dark lanes, Stockport cellars, and St. Ives work-houses, Manchester insurrections, gloomy enough; in France, no great better, daily *émeutes*, kept down by sheer force of armed soldiery; and in this country, following rapidly on in the same way, godless and heartless, sneering at virtue, philanthropy, owning no relation of man to man but what Carlyle terms "cash payment."

What is to be the upshot of all this? Dear countrymen, we have before to-day told you all this; but
though you are wise, intelligent, virtuous—the freest,
noblest, meekest, humblest people that ever breathed
this blessed air of heaven, we see nothing that you
are doing to guard against worse, or to remedy what
is bad. We read the newspapers, the protecting
genii and guardian angels of the land. We seize the
leading editorials, and in the simplicity of our heart
and the eagerness of our spirit ask, What cheer?
Surely, with so many Able Editors, all toiling and
sweating at the anvil, all devoted heart and soul to
the public good, we must be safe, and the means
of averting the calamity dreaded must be within our
reach; the remedy must be found out and insisted
on. Alas! brother editors, we love and honor you;
but we must say, we see not as ye touch the problem,
conceive of it even, far less propose a solution. Ye
are all at work with details, with petty schemes,
proposing nothing that comes up to the mark. Some
of you talk of Home Industry; the wisest among
you talk of Free Trade; none of you, as we hear,
speak of God, and tell your readers that for a people
who worship Mammon, there is no good. Nay, you
must not speak of these matters; for if you do, who
will advertise in your columns or subscribe for your
papers? Nay, how many subscribers will our friend,
the Editor of this Journal, lose by inserting this
very Article? Are we not trenching at every moment
on forbidden ground? Do we say one word that
party leaders will not turn pale or look cross at?
What political capital can be made out of what we
say? Alas! brother editors, do not think we intend

to upbraid you. God knows our condition is not one to be envied. With the whole weight of the republic on our shoulders, and we, alas! none of the strongest in bone or muscle! God pity us! For to carry this huge republic, with its Mammon worships, and its Christian churches reared on traders' shops, and its party strifes, its rush for office, its forgetfulness of man's brotherhood to man, its morality of Let us alone, Save who can, and the devil take the hindmost; workers no longer finding work to do; masterworkers counting their obligations to their workmen discharged in full when the stipulated wages are paid; it is no easy matter.

But, after all, what is the remedy? Let us not deceive ourselves. The whole head is sick, the whole heart is faint. Our industrial arrangements, the relations of master-workers, and workers, of capital and labor, which have grown up during these last three hundred years, are essentially vicious, and, as we have seen, are beginning throughout Christendom to prove themselves so. The great evil is not now in the tyranny or oppression of governments as such; it is not in the arbitrary power of monarchies, aristocracies, or democracies; but it is in the heart of the people, and the industrial order. It is simply, under the industrial head, so far as concerns our material well-being, in this fact, this mournful fact, that there is no longer any certainty of the born worker obtaining always work whereby he can provide for the ordinary wants of a human being. Nor is this altogether the fault of the master-workers. To a very great extent, the immediate employer is himself in turn employed; and as all who produce,

produce to sell, their means of employing, constantly and at reasonable wages, evidently depend on the state of the market; workmen must, therefore, with every depression of trade, be thrown out of employment, whatever the benevolence of the master-workers.

Nor is it possible, with the present organization, or rather *dis*organization of industry, to prevent these ruinous fluctuations of trade. They may undoubtedly be exaggerated by bad legislation, as they may be mitigated by wise and just administration of government, but prevented altogether they cannot be. For this plain reason, that more can be produced, in any given year, with the present productive power, than can be sold in any given five years,—we mean sold to the actual consumer. In other words, by our vicious method of distributing the products of labor, we destroy the possibility of keeping up an equilibrium between production and consumption. We create a surplus—that is a surplus, not when we consider the wants of the people, but when we consider the state of the markets—and then must slacken our hands till the surplus is worked off. During this time, while we are working off the surplus while the mills run short time, or stop altogether, the workmen must want employment. The evil is inherent in the system. We say it is inherent in the *system of wages,* of cash payments, which, as at present understood, the world has for the first time made any general experiment of only now, since the Protestant reformation.

Let us not be misinterpreted. We repeat not here the folly of some men about equality, and every man and even spiritual aspirations, which Christianity teaches us to accept and respect. Much at least of what is most living, least grovelling, least servile, most manly, and most elevated, outside cf the church, is found to-day in their ranks. We are never to judge individual members of political and social parties by their mere doctrinal formulas, for men's heads and hearts are often far apart, and sometimes strongly opposed one to the other. Liberalists and socialists are to be judged, under the point of view we wish now to consider them, not solely nor chiefly by their abstract doctrines, but by their sentiments, their cravings, affections, and aspirations. Liberalism and socialism, like all false systems, end at last in pure gentilism, and yet in their modern form they could have originated only in a community which had once been Christian, and which still retained a tradition of the Christian doctrine of love. They originate in philanthropy, the love of mankind, the form, and the only form, which what is purest and best in religion can assume outside of the Christian church.

We condemn as heartily as any man the liberal and socialistic revolutions of Europe during the last sixty or seventy years, but we cannot deny that those revolutions have to some extent had a philanthropic origin, and have all been prosecuted with the intention of doing for this world by the state through philanthropy what the church has done or shown she can do through Christian charity. All these movements to popularize government, to mitigate penal codes, to redress political and social grievances, and to elevate the poorer and more numerous classes, although for the most part failing in their object, have originated in benevolent sentiment, though perverted to base, selfish purposes by their chief managers. In their writings at least, in their speculations, the philosophers of the last century overflowed with generous sentiments, and if they attacked old systems, and demanded radical changes in social or religious institutions, in laws, manners, and customs, it was always in the name of virtue, and always for the purpose of realizing, as they pretended, often believed, something better for the nation or the race. No small number of the friends and supporters of the old French revolution were moved by a warm and diffusive benevolence; and we envy not the man who can see nothing not bad in the generous enthusiasm of a very considerable portion of the French people in the early days of that revolution. The state of things which obtained in France prior to the revolution was not so bad as that which the revolution itself introduced, but it was such as no man of a sound mind and an honest heart can approve. The evils may have been exaggerated, but no one can deny that they were great and deplorable. The court and upper classes were corrupt either in their principles or their manners, and the great body of the people were oppressed with burdens too heavy to be borne, and looked upon as born only to minister to the wants and pleasures of the idle and luxurious few. How could men who have the hearts of men be otherwise than indignant, when people were sent to the bastile for venturing to attack the king's lackey or the king's mistress,—when the king abandoned himself to the most debasing and criminal sensuality, and a painted harlot, a Pompadour or a Dubarry, was virtually the first minister of state, and dispensed the favors or determined the appointments of the crown, while the toiling multitude were overloaded with taxes, reduced to penury, to absolute destitution, and received in answer to their petition for bread "a new gallows forty feet high"? Revolutions are serious things, and no people can be stirred up to make a social revolution against all that they have been accustomed to hold sacred, till they feel the pressure of want, and see gaunt famine staring them in the face. Nations, humanity at large, must bear some traces of that divine similitude which all things more or less faithfully copy, and can no more act without some aspect of truth or shadow of good than individuals; and though it may be generally more in accordance with the fact to say, *Vox populi vox diaboli,* than *Vox populi vox Dei,* yet there is a sense in which it will not do to deny that "the voice of the people is the voice of God." The old French revolution found at least a pretext in the vices of the court, in the corruption of the noblesse, in the dissoluteness of a portion of the clergy, and in the general neglect and distress of the people. And things were not much worse in France than in other European countries at the same time, if indeed they were so bad. It were idle to deny the existence of the evils, or to hold it to have been criminal, or otherwise than praiseworthy, to attempt to redress them. It was a sacred duty, imposed alike by charity and philanthropy, to undertake their removal, though of course not by unlawful means, certainly not by a revolution, which could only make matters worse.

Of course we have no confidence even in philanthropy, when acting alone, to effect any thing good, for it seldom fails to make matters worse; but we have very little sympathy with the ordinary shallow and selfish declamation of conservatives against modern revolutionary movements. The only conservatism we can respect is that which frankly acknowledges the wrong, and seeks by proper means to redress it wherever it finds it. It is, after all, less against revolutions that we would direct the virtuous indignation of our conservative friends, now that the reaction has become strong, than against the misgovernment, the tyranny, the vices and the crimes, the heartlessness, the cruelty, the neglect of the poor by those who should love and succor them, or the wrongs inflicted on them, which provoke revolutions, and give Satan an opportunity to possess the multitude, and pervert their purest sentiments and their most generous enthusiasm to evil. Revolution was no fitting remedy for the evils which the system of secular government, attained to its full growth in Louis XIV, had generated. It was the remedy of madness or wild despair. But the evils had grown beyond all reasonable endurance. They outraged alike natural benevolence and Christian charity. Let not the friends of religion and order have censures only for these who sought madly to remove them by revolutions, and none for those whose vices and crimes caused them, lest they render religion and order odious to all men of human hearts.

Philanthropy is a human sentiment, and by no means Christian charity. We know it perfectly well. But it corresponds to charity as the human corresponds to the divine, copies it as nature copies or imitates God, and we never need persuade ourselves that what is repugnant to it is pleasing to charity. *Gratia supponit naturam.* How often must we repeat, that grace does not supersede nature? St. Ignatius Loyola did not seek to destroy the natural ambition of young Francis Xavier; he accepted it, and sought simply to direct it from earthly to heavenly glory. No wise master of spiritual life ever seeks to root out nature; his aim is always to accept it, and direct it in right paths towards God, the true end of man. Calvin and Jansenius, those subtle enemies of Christ, have done more injury to religion, a thousand times over, than Voltaire and Rousseau, for they placed nature and grace in opposition, and denied nature in order to assert grace. Not enough have been appreciated the services rendered to religion and humanity by the sons of Loyola, in combating as they did, in the seventeenth century and the beginning of the eighteenth, the degrading and demoralizing, though specious, heresy of the Jansenists. Nobly did they defend the freedom, the dignity, and the glorious destiny of human nature. The infamous *Maxims* of La Rochefoucauld, once so celebrated, were Jansenistic, not Catholic, and were conceived in the spirit of Port Royal, not of the church. They could have been inspired only by a heresy that places grace in opposition to nature, and thinks to exalt the one by degrading and annihilating the other. The Catholic honors nature, and asserts for it a more glorious destiny than do they who madly assert that man in his developments may grow into God. No, we repeat it, God is the similitude of all things, and the human has its type, its exemplar, in the divine. The divine is mirrored, reflected, by the human; grace, therefore, by nature. The natural sentiments of the human heart are below the infused graces of the Christian, but they are not opposed to them. Philanthropy, or the natural benevolence of the human heart, cannot rise to the elevation and power of Christian charity, or aspire to its external reward; but charity no more opposes it, and can no more dispense with it, than revelation opposes or can dispense with reason. What is opposed to benevolence is even more opposed to Christian charity. It is a great mistake to suppose that simple human benevolence or philanthropy is sufficient of itself to redress either social or individual grievances; but it is a still greater mistake therefore to condemn it, to neglect it, to make no efforts to redress the grievances, or to deny them to be real grievances, because they can be effectually redressed only by benevolence exalted to Christian charity. Not all the works of infidels are sin. Works of humanity, of genuine human benevolence, which are not always wanting in non-Catholic society, cannot indeed merit eternal life, or even the grace of conversion, for *gratia est omnio gratis;* but they are not sinful; they are good in the natural order, and merit and shall receive in that order their reward. The men of our times, who have lost the sense of Christian charity and seek to substitute philanthropy for it, do yet honor that charity in its pale and evanescent human reflex, and so far have just sentiments, and are unchristian rather than antichristian.

The doctrine of equal rights, so energetically asserted, a few years since, by "the working-men's party," insisted on under one of its aspects by abolitionists, and by the democratic party throughout the world, is not all false nor all antichristian, and after all faintly mirrors the Christian doctrine of the unity and solidarity of the race. There is truth in the Jacobinical doctrine of "fraternity," and in Kossuth's doctrine of "the solidarity of peoples." The working-men's party is dead now, and buried in other parties which have absorbed it, but it had a great truth for its basis. It asserted the natural nobility of all men, the nobility of human nature itself, as worthy of our reverence in the humble artisan or laborer as in the titled noble.

"The king can make a belted knight,
A marquis, duke, and a' that;
An honest man's aboon his might,
Guid faith! he maunna fa' that."

There is something that it will not do to sneer at in that free and noble spirit that seeks to break down the artificial barriers which separate man from man and nation from nation, and melt all into one grand brotherhood. If there is any one thing certain, it is that the church has always asserted the unity of the race, and the natural equality of all men. Man equals man the world over, and hence, as Pope St. Gregory I teaches, man, though he has received the dominion over the lower creation, has not received dominion over man, and princes are required to govern as pastors, not as lords; for since all men are equal by nature, the governed are as men the equals and brothers of the governors.

We are a little surprised to find the historian of the United States, in his earlier volumes, disposed to regard Calvin as in some sense the champion of equal rights, and to give Calvinism credit for the principle of political equality on which our American institutions are based, for his own doctrine is as repugnant to the Calvinistic, as light is to darkness. Calvinism asserts only a negative equality. It reduces all to a common level, we grant, by asserting the total depravity of nature, and therefore the nullity of nature in all men; but this is the equality of death, noṫ of life. All are equal, because all are nothing. But it does not elevate all to a common level by the assertion of a positive equality, and equality founded on what all men are and have by nature. Moreover, Calvinism is unfavorable, nay, decidedly hostile, to that doctrine of equality which Mr. Bancroft so strenuously maintains. By its doctrine of the nullity of nature and particular election and reprobation, whereby only a certain definite number can be elevated by grace, it founds an aristocracy, the aristocracy of the saints, or the elect. Asserting the moral nullity of nature, it necessarily founds the political order on grace, as it did in Geneva and the early colony of Massachusetts, and excludes from all political rights all whom it does not count among the saints. Maintaining the total depravity of nature, it must deny to nature all rights, and can assert rights only for those who are assumed to be in grace; and hence only the saints have or can have the right to govern,—one of the heresies of Wycliffe, condemned by the Council of Constance. Nature being null, there can be no rights under the law of nature, and if no rights, no possessions. Consequently, they who are counted among the non-elect have nothing which the elect are bound to hold sacred and inviolable. They are at the mercy of the saints, who may at pleasure despoil them of all they call their own, and take possession of their political and civil powers, their houses and lands, their goods and chattels, their wives and children, and even their very persons. Logically and consistently carried out, Calvinism therefore founds, not monarchy indeed, but the aristocracy of the saints, that is, of Calvinists, the most absolute and the most odious aristocracy that it is possible to conceive.

Undoubtedly the regenerate, those who are in grace, alone have rights in regard to eternal salvation, for certainly no man can have a natural right to supernatural beatitude. We are saved not by our natural merits, or merits under the law of nature, but by grace merited for us by Christ our head. The error of the Calvinist does not lie in founding our titles to eternal life on grace and grace alone, but consists in denying the natural law, that man retains all his original rights in the natural order, and that in the natural order all men have equal rights, which even the elect or those elevated by grace must respect as sacred and inviolable. God in promulgating the law of grace does in no respect abrogate the law of nature, nor in the least modify the rights or obligations of men under that law. Hence the apostle recognizes the legitimacy of the temporal power of his time, and bids the faithful to obey for conscience's sake the Roman emperor, though a pagan, in all things temporal. Hence the church recognizes and always has recognized the rights of infidel and even heretical princes to the temporal obedience of their subjects, even when those subjects are Catholics, who can be absolved from their allegiance only in case their princes forfeit their rights *by the law* under which they hold. Hence the church forbids infidels, Jews, or persons who have not come under her spiritual jurisdiction, to be forced to accept the faith. Hence, too, she recognizes the natural rights of life, liberty, and property as fully in infidels and heretics as in the faithful themselves. Here is the grand difference between a positive and a negative natural equality, between the natural equality asserted by Catholicity and that favored by Calvinism. Calvinism asserts the natural equality of all men, by denying alike to all men all natural rights, assuming all rights have been forfeited by the fall; Catholicity asserts the natural equality of all men, by asserting that all have equal natural rights, and denies that any natural rights were forfeited or lost by the transgression of our first parents. The rights lost by the fall were supernatural, not natural rights,—rights held under the law of grace, not rights held under the law of nature; for it was by grace, not nature, that man was placed prior to the fall on the plane of his supernatural destiny. Hence Catholicity recognizes in nature something sacred and inviolable, which even the church must respect. Hence Catholicity must always respect the natural liberty of man, and can no more tyrannize over the infidel than over the believer,—must, in fact, as to the natural order, place both on the same footing of equality. Calvinism begins by denying all natural rights, nullifying nature, and therefore all natural liberty, and asserts rights for the elect only. Hence it is free from all obligation to the non-elect, that is, to those who are not Calvinists, and is at liberty to play the tyrant over them at pleasure.

This is not mere speculation, or a simple logical conclusion from the Calvinistic premises. It is a conclusion practically drawn by Calvinists themselves, and written out in the blood of non-Calvinists, wherever they have had the power. Never have Calvinists held sacred any liberty except liberty for Calvinists. You may verify the fact by the history of Calvinism in Geneva, by that of the Puritans in England, that of the Covenanters in Scotland, and that of our own Puritan ancestors. Liberty for the elect, but no liberty for the non-elect, is the Calvinistic motto. To the saints belongs the earth. Do you not see this in the Know-Nothing movement against Catholics in our own country? Unbelievers, Unitarians, Universalists, and non-Evangelical sects, may engage in that movement, but its informing and controlling spirit is that of Calvinism, just now galvanized into a sort of spasmodic life. Its very language betrays it. It professes religious liberty, and its very aim is to deny it to Catholics, who in its view, we suppose are reprobates.

We may see here, again, the title of the Jesuits, as true Catholics, to the gratitude of mankind, for the noble energy with which they vindicated the rights and dignity of nature against insidious Jansenism, that improved edition of Calvanism. "Nature," as some one remarks, "is not good for nothing." It is not good for everything, yet it is good for something, and in its place is no more to be denied than grace itself.

That Calvinism has accidentally served the cause of equal rights in this country we are not disposed to deny. It led our Calvinistic ancestors to assert equal rights for the elect, that is, for Calvinists, and to make provisions for protecting them. When Calvinism lost its sway, and had become, as it practically had at the time of the revolution, a dead letter, these provisions were without much difficulty extended so as to apply equally to all citizens, elect or non-elect. But no thanks to Calvinism for that, for they were so extended and made to protect equal rights, not as rights of the elect, but as the rights of man. We think, if Mr. Bancroft had studied more thoroughly the Calvinistic system, he would have seen that, of all conceivable systems, it is the least favorable to that liberty and equality which he so eloquently and so energetically asserts. The equality that results from the equal depravity of nature can never be the basis of the equal rights of all men. To obtain this basis you must assert with the Catholic the inherent freedom, dignity, and nobility of human nature in every man, which requires the assertion of the unity of the race, and the recognition of that great fact, so seldom reflected on, so little understood, and so seldom practically applied, that God made man in his own image and likeness, and therefore man in his very nature must copy, imitate, or mirror his Maker.

The working-men were right in asserting the natural equality, or equal natural rights, of all men, and even in asserting the equal natural rights of all men to means and facilities for acquiring: for they did not, as it was alleged, assert the natural right of all men to equal acquisitions. The inequality they complained of was the unequal condition in which men are artificially placed in regard to acquiring, whether it be riches or honors, power or profit. Their error was in seeking to remove this inequality by social or political action. This inequality is, no doubt, in regard to the temporal order, a real grievance; but the difficulty is that it cannot be redressed by society, or if it can, not without striking at the right of property, and thus producing a far greater evil. There are many things very desirable, very proper to be done, which exceed both the ability and the competency of the state to do. The state alone is not competent to all the wants of even natural society. It must protect acquired as well as natural rights, and therefore the right to hold as well as to acquire property; and if it does this, it cannot secure to every man equal means or facilities for acquiring. It is obliged by its very nature to content itself with maintaining the equal right of all to acquire, and to hold what they acquire; when more is needed, we must look to a power of another order,—the moral power. The working-men committed a mistake analogous to that committed by our ultra-temperance people. Intemperance is a sin, a vice, which every man ought to avoid, and temperance is a virtue which every man ought to practise. But the state is competent in the case only to leave full freedom to the virtue, and to punish the intemperance only in so far as it deprives some one of his rights. In that it is a sin or a vice, the state is not competent to deal with it, either by way of prevention or of punishment; it can take cognizance of it only in that it is an injury, or deprives some one of his rights, natural or acquired. The state cannot punish the simple vice of drunkenness; it can punish drunkenness only when it interferes with the rights of others, or disturbs the public peace. Hence the principle of the Maine liquor law is indefensible. A man has a natural right to drink wine, beer, cider, gin, rum, brandy, or whiskey, if he chooses, and can honestly procure it. He has a right to use intoxicating drinks so long as he does not abuse them. That right is and must be sacred and inviolable for the state. The state can have the right to deal only with the abuse. But the Maine liquor law proceeds on the principle that the state has the right to guard against the abuse by prohibiting the use, or by declaring the use itself an abuse. This, as it assumes for the state the right to alter the moral law or to introduce a new principle into morals, cannot be admitted, unless we are prepared to assert civil despotism. The office of the state is not to teach morals, or to interpret the moral law, but to execute it; not to define right, but to protect and vindicate it. To teach morals, to define what is or is not right, is not within the competency of the civil power. That belongs to the spiritual or moral power, distinct from the civil power, and moving in another orbit. The equality, if the working-men had understood it, which they wanted, they would have sought from love, not law, and by means of the church, not the state; for the church alone can introduce equality in the matters of acquired rights, by teaching the doctrine of love, and bringing home to the consciences of rich possessors, that they are stewards, and not absolute proprietors, of their estates, and therefore are to use them for the good of their neighbor, not for their own private good alone, on the principle that each is bound for all and all for each, or that all are members of one body, and members of one another, and that the body cannot suffer without the members, nor a member without the body. It was on this principle that St. Chrysostom told the rich of Constantinople that they were murderers of the poor who died for the want of the means wherewith to live. But it would be perfect madness to attempt to carry out this principle by political organization or legislative action. The right to acquire and to hold property independent of the civil power must be recognized and protected, or the whole community will die of starvation. The evil which the state must tolerate for the sake of the good, the moral power operating on conscience and love must redress.

The doctrine of the solidarity and communion of the race, which Leroux makes the basis of his socialism and the principle of his explanation of Christianity, has something which, perhaps, a Christian may, and even must, accept. If we may be permitted to refer to our personal experience, we must say that it was through that doctrine, as set forth by Leroux in his work on *Humanity,* that by the grace of God we were led to the Catholic Church; and we may add, that the same was true of several of our friends, one at least of whom is now a most worthy member of the Catholic priesthood, and one of the most indefatigable and successful Catholic missionaries in the country. We thought we saw a great and important truth in the doctrine, but also that, as Leroux laid it down, it was incomplete; and if theoretically and practically completed anywhere, it must be in the Catholic Church. We seized the doctrine with our accustomed ardor, and, developing it in our own way, found ourselves knocking at the door of the church, and demanding entrance. Having been admitted into the church, and commenced the study of Catholic theology in the scholastic authors, in whom we found nothing which seemed to us a recognition of it, we felt that it was our duty to waive its public consideration till we could have time and opportunity of reëxamining it in the light of Catholic faith. We saw at once that the doctrine pertained to an order of thought far below Catholic dogma, and that we had erred in supposing it to be the explication and expression of the real sense of the Catholic mysteries; but how far it was or was not in harmony with them, we felt unable to say. It was a problem to be solved, and not by us till we had become somewhat more familiar than we were at the time with Catholic theology. The form under which we had entertained it was, in regard to scholastic theology, a novelty, and therefore to be suspected. It might conceal an error, and even a dangerous error. It was certainly prudent, nay, it was our duty, not to insist on it, and to be content with using the language, arguments, and illustrations which we knew to be safe. Hence the trains of thought with which we made our readers so familiar during our transition state, and which had played so important a part in the process of our conversion, were suddenly interrupted the moment we entered the church and began to write as a Catholic. They who have watched our course, and taken some

interest in our progress from a low form of rational-
ism to Catholicity, were unable to trace in our writings any continuity of thought between what was
published the day before we entered the church and
what we wrote and published the day after. So
abrupt and complete a change seemed to them in-
explicable on any rational principles, and was of
course ascribed to our fickleness, or to our no longer
being suffered to have a mind of our own. People
outside of the church lost confidence in us, and if
they continued to read us at all, it was mainly to
amuse themselves with what they were pleased to
look upon as our "feats of intellectual gladiatorship."
This of course had its unpleasantness and its incon-
veniences, but it was not unendurable.

But we may say now, after more than ten years
of silent thought and reflection on the subject, that,
though not free from trifling errors, and much exaggerated as to their importance in our own mind, the
principles which we learned from Leroux and developed and applied in our own way were substantially
true, and we can without lesion to our Catholicity
resume the train of thought which appeared to be
so abruptly terminated on our entering the church.
The views which we set forth in our Letter to Dr.
Channing, in 1842, *on the Mediatorial Life of
Jesus,** as far as they went, we can accept now, and
not without advantage. They were not what we
thought them, and did not attain, as we supposed, to
Catholic doctrine; yet they embraced elements of
natural truth which help us in some respects to understand the Catholic dogma, and which the dogma

* Vol. IV., p. 140.

may accept as charity accepts philanthropy. The basis of the doctrine we set forth in that letter was, that man lives by communion with God, humanity, and nature, and that his life partakes of the qualities of the object with which he communes. Man cannot live by himself alone, and every fact of life is the resultant of two factors, of the concurrent activity of subject and object, and partakes of the character of each. The individual can live and act only by virtue of communion with that which is not himself, and which we call his object, because it is set over against him. This does not mean that he cannot act without some object, or end to which he acts, although that is undoubtedly the case, but without another activity than his own, which meets and concurs with it. The fact of life results from the inter-shock of the two activities, and is their joint product. The subject is *living* subject, or subject *in actu,* only by virtue of communion with its object. Thus it cannot think without the active presence of the intelligible, or love without the active presence of the amiable, which is really only what St. Thomas teaches when he says the intellect is *in ordine ad verum,* and the will *in ordine ad bonum;* that the intellect is never false, and the will can will only good. Therefore we have frequently brought out the doctrine in order to refute the modern psychologists, and those philosophers who would persuade us that it is not the *mundus physicus,* but an intermediary world, which they call the *mundus logicus,* that the mind in its perceptions immediately apprehends. The mind cannot think without thinking some object, and as to the production of thought, the object must act on or with the subject,—because if purely passive it is as if it were not, for pure passivity is mere potentiality,—the object must be real, being or existence, since what neither is nor exists cannot act or produce any effect. Consequently, either we perceive nothing and perform no act of perception, or the world perceived is the real world itself, not a merely abstract or logical world, or a mere *species* or phantasm.

But thought is an effect, and whoever thinks at all produces or generates something. Every theologian must admit this, or how else can he hold the mystery of the Trinity, and believe in the only begotten Son of God? In God, who is *actus purissimus,* or pure act, as say Aristotle and the schoolmen after him, as he is infinite and contains no passivity, he enters with his whole being into his thought, the word generated is and must be exactly his equal, and identical in nature, consubstantial with himself. But man, not being pure act, nor intelligible in himself, cannot think without another activity that supplies the object necessary to reduce his passivity to act; and as he cannot enter with his whole being into his thought, he cannot, as God, generate the exact image of himself. Nevertheless, in conjunction with the object, since he imitates in his degree the divine intellect, he generates something, and this something we call a fact of life, or life itself considered as the product of living activity. Now, since the production or generation of thought or the fact of life subject and object must concur, it is their joint product, and must participate of the character of each. Here is the basis of what is called the solidarity of the race, under the point of view of intellect.

But man is not pure intellect. He has a heart as well as a head, and can love as well as think. What we have asserted of thought is equally true of love, as we learn from the same adorable mystery of the Trinity. For the Father, the unbegotten, loves the Son, the begotten, and from their mutual love proceeds the third person of the Trinity, the Holy Ghost. Only like can commune with like, and love properly so called can be only of like to like, and therefore under the relation of love man only can be the object of man. By virtue of the unity of the race every human being is the object of every other human being. But by the law of all communion of subject and object, the result generated or proceeding is the joint product of the two factors, and therefore the life of any one man is the joint product of him and every other man; and thus is produced a solidarity of the life of all men, by which it is one and the same life for all and for each, and for each and for all. But as every generation, so to speak, overlaps its successor, and each new generation communes with its predecessor, the solidarity of the race is not only a solidarity of all men in space, but of all men in time, linking together, in one indissoluble life, the first man with the last, and the last man with the first.

Taking this doctrine, but giving a different application from that of Leroux, in order to escape his denial of the personality of God and the personal immortality of the soul, and to be able to assert the Incarnation in the individual man Jesus, instead of the race, we thought we could bridge over the gulf between the Unitarian and the Trinitarian, and accept and explain the Christian church and Christian mysteries. In this respect our letter to Dr. Channing fails. The thought we developed does not rise to the order of Catholic dogma, and at the highest remains in the natural order. Yet the doctrine is substantially true. It is not the supernatural truth of Christianity, but it is in some sense the truth of the natural order which corresponds to it, and by which it is made apprehensible to us. The error of Leroux and ourselves was not in asserting the natural communion and solidarity of the race, but in supposing them to be the real significance of the Christian mysteries, the Incarnation, Holy Communion, the Church, Apostolic Succession, Tradition, &c., or the great truths held by the early Christians, and symbolized by the Catholic dogmas. The error was in assuming that Catholic dogmas symbolize natural truths; it had been more correct to have said the reverse, that the natural truths symbolize the dogmas, or represent them as the human represents the divine. "See that you make all things according to the pattern shown you in the Mount." The earthly symbolizes the heavenly, not the heavenly the earthly. The dogma is not, as Leroux, Cousin, and others have foolishly asserted, the form with which faith, the religious sentiment, or enthusiasm, clothes the natural or philosophic truth. The natural or philosophic truth, on the contrary, is the symbol of which the dogma is the hidden meaning, the divine reality, or the divine likeness which it copies or imitates.

Although the natural communion of the human race does not introduce us to the principle of the sacraments, as Leroux and we after him supposed, and although the natural solidarity of the race is

infinitely below the Christian solidarity effected by
the sacraments, there is no opposition between one
and the other. We do not by natural communion
receive and incorporate into our life that grace which
unites us to God and enables us to live the supernatural life of Christ, and the solidarity resulting
from it is infinitely below that of the church, that
mystic body of Christ, in which he is as it were con-
tinuously incarnated; but it does express the condition of our natural human life, and its assertion,
while no disadvantage to the supernatural, is of great
advantage to the natural order. It condemns all ex-
clusiveness, whether individual or national, and
asserts the necessity to the full development of our
natural life of the free and peaceful intercourse of
man with man the world over. Man has a threefold
nature, and lives by communion with God, man, and
nature. He communes with God in religion, with
man in society, and with nature in property, and any
political or social order that strikes at either of these,
or hinders or obstructs this threefold communion, as
Leroux well maintains, is alike repugnant to the will
of God and the highest interests of humanity; and
efforts made to render this communion free and
unobstructed, to give freedom in the acquisition and
security in the possession of property, to protect
the family as the basis of society, and to break down
the barriers to social intercourse interposed by prej-
udices of birth or caste, and to secure freedom of
worship or religion, are in principle great and solemn
duties, obligatory alike upon all men. Thus far
the liberalists and socialists can make a valid defence. The end proposed is just and obligatory. The

means they adopt of course we do and must condemn. Philanthropy enjoins what they would effect, and philanthropy here may justify herself by the natural solidarity of the race.

Kossuth, when he was here, had much to say of "the solidarity of peoples," from which he concluded the right of the people of every country, irrespective of their government, to run to the assistance of any particular people struggling for its rights. This solidarity of peoples rests on the doctrine of the solidarity of the race. Man lives his social life only by communion with man, and every man thus becomes every man's object, and all are bound together in the unity of one indissoluble life. Man then can never be indifferent to man; never have the right to ask, with Cain, "Am I my brother's keeper?" Your brother is your object, without which you cannot live the life of love. He is your other self, the objective side of your own life. If this may be said of individuals, why not of nations? There is in some sense a solidarity of nations, as well as individuals. The right of the people without the permission of their government to assist a sister people, we cannot absolutely deny. The race is more than the individual, and humanity more than the nation. There is a great and glorious truth in Senator Seward's doctrine of the higher law, a truth which every true man will assert, if need be, in exile or the dungeon, on the scaffold or at the stake. I am a man before I am a citizen, and my rights as a man can never be subordinated to my duties as a citizen. Even the church recognizes and vindicates my rights as a man, and the church is higher in the order of God's providence than the state, as much so as grace is higher than nature. There are cases in which the state cannot bind the citizen, as the apostles taught us when they refused to obey the magistrates who commanded them to preach no more in the name of Jesus of Nazareth. We are to love our neighbor as ourself; for in one sense our neighbor is ourself, since he is our object, without which we cannot love or live; there are cases when we must rush to his assistance, at least when we *may* rush to his assistance, at the hazard of life. There may then be cases when the solidarity of the race overrides the solidarity of the nation, and permits a people without the national sanction to rush to the assistance of another people struggling against tyranny for its liberty and independence; but not indeed at the call of every discomfited demagogue. The principle we hold to be true, but it can be of only rare application. The struggling people must have a cause manifestly just, and have adopted means manifestly unexceptionable, and the national permission must have been wrongly withheld, before the people of another nation have the right to interfere; and these things must be determined not by private judgment or caprice, but by an authority competent to decide in the case, otherwise an attack may be made against legitimate authority, and a blow be struck at order, which is as sacred as liberty.

We might pursue this subject further, but it is unnecessry at present. We have thus far been intent mainly on pointing out what a Catholic may accept as true and good in modern liberalism and socialism. What they want, we mean when sincere, earnest, and disinterested, what they are driving at, under certain aspects, is good, and in its place approved alike by charity and philanthropy. We cannot utterly condemn all we did and said as a liberalist or as a socialist, and we find much in liberalists and socialists of the present day to approve. When they are not completely beside themselves, we admit that most of the things they call political and social grievances are grievances, and such as ought to be redressed. But with what they contend for that is true and good, they couple great and dangerous errors. They err, above all, as to the means by which they seek to gain their ends. In what they for the most part aim at, we can agree with them. We love liberty as much as they do, we are as indignant at wrong as they are; but we see them trying to effect by the state what can be effected only by the church, and by the natural sentiment of philanthropy what is practicable only by the supernatural virtue of charity.

Every age has its own characteristics, and we must address its dominant sentiment, whether we would serve or disserve it. Our age is philanthropical rather than intellectual. It has lost faith intellectually, but retains a faint echo of it on the side of the affections. It does not think so much as it feels, and it demands the gospel of love with far more earnestness and energy than it does the gospel of truth. Charity had exalted and intensified its affections. Despoiled of charity, it is devoured by its benevolent sentiments. It would do good, it would devote itself to the poor, the enslaved, the neglected, the downtrodden. It would bind up the broken heart, and bring rest to the suffering. These are not bad traits, and we love to dwell on the disinterestedness of the Howards, the Frys, the Nightingales, and the benevolent men and women in our own country who so unreservedly devote themselves to the relief of the afflicted. These prove what the age craves, and what it is looking for. Through its benevolence Satan no doubt often misleads it, but through the same benevolence the missionary of the cross may approach it and lead it up to God.

We have wished, in these times, when the church is assailed so violently by the galvanized Calvinism manifesting itself in Know-Nothing movements, to show, by exhibiting the manner in which she regards those movements which spring from natural benevolence or a generous regard for human well-being, that she no more deserves than she fears their violence. What is true and good in the natural order manifested by those outside, though imperfect, she accepts. We have wished, also, in a practical way, to reply to those who are perpetually accusing us of being narrow and exclusive, and a renegade from free principles. What we aimed at before our conversion is still dear to us, and we are still in some sense a man of our age. But having indicated the good side of liberalism and socialism, we shall take a future opportunity to show more fully that it is accepted by the church, and is completed only in and through her communion.

CHAPTER FOUR

LIBERALISM AND PROGRESS*

NOTE ON "LIBERALISM AND PROGRESS"

Written while the outcome of the Civil War still was in question, this essay (published in *Brownson's Quarterly Review* for October, 1864) is a good example of Orestes Brownson's resolute candor. An unflinching supporter of the Union, he does not hesitate, for all that, to declare his preference for Southern society and his detestation of vulgar democratic dogmas, the gospel of material success, and radical notions of human progress. Brownson looked upon the terrible struggle between North and South as a contrast between just authority and the anarchic impulse, not a doctrinaire crusade of democratic ideologists against a conservative society. Here Brownson makes the most penetrating analysis of real American conservatism, in a few thousand words, in the whole of our political literature. He flays the liberal tendency to create wants beyond the possibility of satisfaction, and protests that constitutions founded upon mere consent of the governed lack that divine sanction which is the spring of justice and of peace.

* * *

[From *Brownson's Quarterly Review* for October, 1864.]

This work, which has not yet found a publisher, and which exists only in the author's autograph, has come honestly into our possession, with permission to make such use of it as we see proper. The author

---

* *Tendencies of Modern Society, with Remarks on the American People, Government, and Military Administration.* BY GENERAL CROAKER. MS.

seems to have been only a civilian general, as his name does not appear in the army Register, and we suspect that he has never served in any army, hardly in a band of filibusters. From his English, and his inability to see any thing in our habits or manners, in our civil or military service, to commend, we should judge him some disappointed foreigner, who at the breaking out of our civil war, had offered his services to the government and had them refused. He regards himself as qualified for any post from pathmaster to president, or from corporal to commander-in-chief of the armies of the United States, which makes against the theory that he is a foreigner, and would indicate that he is a native, and "to the manner born." He finds every thing amiss with us, and that things can come right only by his being placed at the head of our civil and military affairs.

The general (?) is very profuse in his military criticisms, and shows a very hostile spirit towards our military academy. He blames the government for intrusting important commands to men who have been educated at West Point, and insists that if it will appoint Americans to the commands of its armies, it should appoint civilians, who have not been narrowed, belittled, and cramped by the pedantry of a military education. He prefers instinct to study, and the happy inspirations of ignorance to the calculations of science. He thinks our true course is to invite hither the military adventurers so numerous on the continent of Europe, and who can find, in consequence of their devotion to democracy, no employment at home, and give them the command of our armies. He does not seem to be aware that we have tried his theory pretty thoroughly in both respects, and have found it not to work well. We passed in the beginning over the army, and made nearly all our high military appointments from civil life. In our first batch of major-generals, not one was taken from the army, and only one was taken who had been educated at West Point. The government commenced with as great a distrust of West Point and a military education and military experience, and with as great a confidence in the military instincts and inspirations of civilians or political aspirants, as our author himself could desire, and with what wisdom the country knows, to its sorrow. Most of our civilian generals have proved sad failures; West Point is now at a premium, and would remain so, but for the wretched policy of making most new appointments in the army from the ranks, thereby spoiling good sergeants and making poor officers. Something besides bravery even is demanded of an officer. Gentlemanly tastes, habits, education, and manners, a knowledge of his profession, and an aptitude to command men, are necessary. Appointments from the ranks, as a reward of extraordinary merit, is well; but they should be sparingly and judiciously made. When we make appointments from the ranks the rule, they cease to be the reward of merit, and degrade the army and impair its efficiency.

In the beginning of the war, we had almost any number of foreign adventurers in our service, but we have been obliged to get rid of the larger portion of them. Some among the foreign officers who have received commissions from our government are men of real merit, and have served with intelligence and success; but the majority of them have proved to be men "who left their country for their country's good." No national army can be worth any thing that is to any considerable extent officered by foreigners. If the nation cannot from itself officer its own army, it had better not go to war; for it is pretty sure to fail if it does. Then war as made here assumes a peculiar character. Carried on over our vast extent of country, much of it either a wilderness, or sparingly settled, in a manner so different from what the training and experience acquired in European armies and wars fit one for, that foreign officers can be of little use to us. Neither the strategy nor the tactics of a Napoleon would secure success here. The men who enter a foreign service are, besides, rarely the best officers in the army of their native country, and are usually such as their own government does not care to employ. We maintain, too, that though West Point is susceptible of improvement, nowhere are young men better trained for the profession of arms, and it is very little that the men from abroad, who seek commissions in our army, can teach our West Pointers. The great objection to our army officers at the opening of the war was their lack of experience in commanding, moving, and manœuvring large bodies of men; but the foreigners who seek to enter our armies equally lack that experience. They have had only a lieutenant's, a captain's, a major's, or at most a colonel's command in their own country, or in the foreign service to which they had been attached. At the opening of the war, there were some who were mad enough to wish the government to invite Garibaldi to come and take command of our army; but Garibaldi, however successful he might have been as the tool of Piedmont or Mazzini in stirring up insurrection, and as a partisan commander, never commanded nor proved himself capable of commanding an army of thirty thousand men. Besides, his proper place in this country would not have been in the federal army, but in that of the rebels. To fight against rebellion and revolution in defence of legal authority and established government would have been a novelty to him, and contrary to his native instincts.

Our author is a decided democrat, in the European sense of the word, and complains that the American people are not truly and thoroughly democratic. He has no sympathy with our people, and thinks them false to their own democratic principles. What brought him here, if a foreigner, and induced him to offer us his valuable services, which appear to have been rejected, was his sympathy with democracy, and hostility to all other actual or possible forms of government. He wanted to sustain democracy here, not for our sake, but as a *point d'appue* for his operations against monarchy and aristocracy in Europe. All this may be very well in him, only he is on the wrong side, as would have been his friend Garibaldi. The struggle in which we are engaged, notwithstanding what some silly journalists write and publish, is not a struggle for the triumph of democracy. So to understand it is to misunderstand it; and we always regret to find friends of the Union urging the war as a war between the northern democracy and the southern aristocracy. Such many have tried and are still trying to make it; but such is not its real legitimate character. On our side it is a war in defence of government, of authority, and the supremacy of law. It is a war in vindication of national integrity, and in defence of American constitutionalism. The very thing our author would have us make the principle and end of the war, is that which the war is waged against. We wish to abolish slavery as far as it can be done without appealing to humanitarian or revolutionary principles: but we have neither the right nor the wish to seek to revolutionize southern society. Politically, southern society is no more aristocratic in its constitution than northern society: if socially it is more so, that is an advantage, not a disadvantage. In the present struggle, southern society has proved relatively stronger and more energetic than northern society, because in southern society the people are marshalled under their natural leaders, under men who are intrinsically superior to the mass, and felt to be so; while in the northern states they have been marshalled under no leaders or under artificial leaders, not superior, and often inferior, to those they are commissioned to lead. No society that has not a natural aristocracy, if we may borrow a phrase from Thomas Jefferson, has any really cohesive power, or any more strength than a rope of sand.

We have some madmen amongst us who talk of exterminating the southern leaders, and of new-englandizing the South. We wish to see the free-labor system substituted for the slave-labor system, but beyond that we have no wish to exchange or modify southern society, and would rather approach northern society to it, than it to northern society. The New Englander has excellent points, but is restless in body and mind, always scheming, always in motion, never satisfied with what he has, and always seeking to make all the world like himself, or as uneasy as himself. He is smart, seldom great; educated, but seldom learned; active in mind, but rarely a profound thinker; religious, but thoroughly materialistic: his worship is rendered in a temple founded on Mammon, and he expects to be carried to heaven in a softly-cushioned railway car, with his sins carefully checked and deposited in the baggage crate with his other luggage, to be duly delivered when he has reached his destination. He is philanthropic, but makes his philanthropy his excuse for meddling with everybody's business as if it were his own, and under pretence of promoting religion and morality, he wars against every generous and natural instinct, and aggravates the very evils he seeks to cure. He has his use in the community; but a whole nation composed of such as he would be short-lived, and resemble the community of the lost rather than that of the blest. The Puritan is a reformer by nature, but he never understands the true law of progress, and never has the patience to wait till the reform he wishes for can be practically effected. He is too impatient for the end ever to wait the slow operations of the means, and defeats his own purpose by his inconsiderate haste. He needs the slower, the more deliberate, and the more patient and enduring man of the South to serve as his counterpoise.

The South has for its natural leaders, not simply men of property, but men of large landed estates, and who are engaged in agricultural pursuits: the North has for its natural leaders business men and their factors, who may or may not be men of wealth, or who, if rich to-day, may be poor to-morrow, and who necessarily seek to subordinate every thing to business interests. They of course are less fitted, in a country like ours, to lead than the landholders, because agriculture with us is a broader and more permanent interest of the nation than trade or manufactures.

We insist that it were a gross perversion of the war to make it a war against Southern society or the Southern people. The war is just and defensible only when it is conducted as a war of the nation for its own existence and rights against an armed rebellion. In the war the nation seeks to reduce the rebels to their allegiance, not to destroy them, not to exile them, not to deprive them of their property or their franchise; it seeks to make them once more loyal citizens, and an integral portion of the American people, standing on a footing of perfect equality with the rest, not slaves or tributaries. Southern society must be respected, and any attempt to build up a new South out of the few Union men left there, northern speculators, sharpers, adventurers, and freed negroes, is not only impolitic, but unconstitutional and wrong. Such a South would be a curse to itself and to the whole nation; we want it not. With here and there an individual exception, the real people of the South are united in the rebellion, and under their natural leaders, and any scheme of settlement that does not contemplate their remaining with their natural leaders, the real, substantial, ruling people of the southern states, will not only fail, but ought not to be entertained. They must have the control of affairs in their respective states, and represent them in the councils of the nation. The nation cannot afford to lose them; if it could, it need not have gone to war against them. The bringing of the negro element, except in states where it is too feeble to amount to any thing, into American political society will never be submitted to by either the North or the South. We must suppress the rebellion; but with the distinct understanding that the southern states are to be restored, when they submit, to all the rights of self-government in the Union, and that no attempt in the mean time shall be made to revolutionize their society in favor of northern or European ideas. If in our haste, our wrath, or our zeal we have said any thing that can bear a different sense, it must be retracted.

Friends of constitutional government, and of liberty with law, may justly sympathize with our government in the present struggle; but not European radicals, democrats, and revolutionists, for the principle of the struggle is as hostile to them as it is to the southern rebels. In this war the nation is fighting northern democracy or Jacobinism as much as it is southern aristocracy, and the evidence of it is in the fact, that the people cease to support willingly the war just in proportion as it assumes a Jacobinical character, and loses its character of a war in defence of government and law. The administration may not see it; and the philosophers of the *New York Tribune* and *Evening Post,* well convinced as they may be that something is wrong, may deny it, and propose to cure the evil by doubling the dose of radicalism; even the people, while they instinctively feel, may not be fully aware that it is that which holds them back; but so it is, and nothing for years has given us so much hope for our country as this very fact. It proves that, after all, the popular instincts are right, and that while the people are ready to carry on a war to preserve the constitution and government, they are not prepared to carry on a war for revolutionizing either. These foreign radicals and revolutionists who complain of our democracy, that it is not thorough-going and consistent, and does not press straight to its end, ought to understand that there is no legitimate sympathy between them and us, and that they cannot fight their battles in ours. We are not fighting their battles, and those of our countrymen who think we are, begin already to find themselves deserted by the nation. The American people, however ready they have been to sympathize with revolution, and encourage insurrection and rebellion in foreign nations, therein imitating the English Whigs, are yet very far from being revolutionists in the interior of their souls, and for their own country.

Our author, who professes to side with the Federalists, keeps an eye on the revolutionary movements in Europe, and a considerable part of his work is written with the express intention of forwarding them. He rejoices at the spread of democratic ideas in England, in Germany, and in Italy, and he expresses his hope that the democratic party will rise again in France, and hurl the emperor from his throne. We trust we love liberty and free government as much as does this disappointed foreigner, or American with foreign sympathies and notions: but, in our judgment, what Europe most wants at present is repose in the interior of her several nations, and freedom for their respective governments to devote themselves to the welfare and progress of the people, for which they can do nothing, so long as they have to use all their power and energy to maintain their own existence. Every enlightened well-wisher to European society would rejoice to see the whole race of European revolutionists exterminated, or converted into loyal and peaceful subjects. True liberty was never yet advanced by subverting the established government of a country. Europe has lost far more than it has gained by its century of insurrections, revolutions, and civil wars, and the new *régimes* introduced have left fewer effective guaranties of civil freedom and personal liberty than existed before them. Providence may overrule evil for good, but good is never the natural product of evil.

We know, in censuring the revolutionary spirit of modern society, we are placing ourselves in opposition to the whole so-called liberal party of the civilized world; but that is not our fault. The liberal party so called has its good side and its bad side. Some things in it are to be commended, and other things in it, whoever would not stultify himself must condemn. Man is by nature a social being, and cannot live and thrive out of society; society is impracticable without strong and efficient government; and strong and efficient government is impracticable, where the people have no loyal sentiments, and hold themselves free to make war on their government and subvert it whenever they please. Men and governments, no doubt, are selfish, and prone to abuse power when they have it; but no government can stand that rests only on the selfishness of the human heart, or on what in the last century they called "enlightened self-interest," *l'intérêt bien entendu,* and not on the sense of duty, strengthened by loyal affection. People must feel not only that it is their interest to sustain government, but that it is their moral and religious duty to sustain it; and when they have no moral sense, no religion, and no loyal affection, they should know that they cannot sustain it, and society must cease to exist. A nation of atheists were a solecism in history. A few atheists may, perhaps, live in society, and even serve it for a time, where the mass of the people are believers and worshippers, but an entire nation of real atheists was never yet founded, and never could subsist any longer than it would take to dissipate the moral wealth acquired while it was as yet a religious nation. It was well said by the Abbé de La Mennais, before his unhappy fall: "Religion is always found by the cradle of nations, philosophy only at their tombs"— meaning, as he did, philosophy in the sense of unbelief and irreligion; not philosophy in the sense of the rational exercise of the faculties of the human mind on divine and human things, aided by the light of revelation. The ancient lawgivers always sought for their laws not only a moral, but a religious sanction, and where the voice of God does not, in some form, speak to men's consciences, and bid them obey the higher power, government can subsist only as a craft or as sheer force, which nobody is bound to respect or obey.

The great misfortune of modern liberalism is, that it was begotten of impatience and born of a reaction against the tyranny and oppression, the licentiousness and despotism of governments and the governing classes; and it is more disposed to hate than to love, and is abler to destroy than to build up. Wherever you find it, it bears traces of its origin, and confides more in human passion than in divine Providence. The great majority of its adherents, even if they retain a vague and impotent religious sentiment, and pay some slight outward respect to the religion of their country, yet place the state above the church, the officers of government above the ministers of religion, and maintain that priests have nothing to do with the affairs of this world. They forget that it is precisely to introduce the elements of truth, justice, right, duty, conscience into the government of individuals and nations in this world, as the means of securing the next, that institutions of religion exist, and priests are consecrated. Politicians may do as they please, so long as they violate no rule of right, no principle of justice, no law of God; but in no world, in no order, in no rank, or condition, have men the right to do wrong. Religion, if any thing is the *lex suprema,* and what it forbids, no man has the right to do. This is a lesson liberalism has forgotten, or never learned.

In our last *Review* we defended civil and religious freedom and pointed out to the *obscurantists* in church and state, wherein and wherefore they mistake this age, are laboring for an impossibility, and fail to recall men to faith, and to reëstablish in its integrity the unity of Christendom; but whoever inferred from what we then said that we have any sympathy with political atheism, reasoned from premises of his own, not from any we ever laid down or entertained. Almost entire volumes of this *Review* are filled with refutations, such as they are, of political atheism, and the defence of the authority of religion for the human conscience in all the affairs of human life. There are elements in modern liberaiism that it will not do to oppose, because, though liberalism misapplies them, they are borrowed from the Gospel, are taken from Christian civilization, and are, in themselves, true, noble, just, and holy. Nor can we recall modern society to that old order of things, that liberalism began by opposing, even if it were desirable, which it is not. Many things we may seek to save from being overthrown, which, when overthrown, it would be madness to attempt to reëstablish. But we have never denied that modern liberalism has an odor of infidelity and irreligion, and assumes an independence of religion, that is, of conscience, of God, which is alike incompatible with the salvation of souls and the progress of society. Liberals, if they would study the question, would soon find that religion offers no obstacle to any thing true and good they wish to effect, and even offers them that very assistance without which they cannot effect or preserve it.

It is the mad attempt to separate the progress of society from religion that has rendered modern liberalism everywhere destructive, and everywhere a failure. It has sapped the foundation of society, and rendered government, save as a pure despotism, impracticable, by taking from law its sacredness, and authority its inviolability, in the understanding and consciences of men. The world, since the opening of modern history, in the fifteenth century, has displayed great activity, and in all directions; but its progress in the moral and intellectual orders has been in losing rather than in gaining. Its success in getting rid of old ideas, old beliefs, old doctrines, old sentiments, old practices, and in cutting itself loose from all its old moorings, has been marvellous, and well-nigh complete. Taste has, indeed, been refined, and manners, habits, and sentiments have been softened, and become more humane, but we have not learned that they have gained much in purity or morality. There has been a vast development of material resources, great progress in the application of science to the productive arts, and a marvellous augmentation of material goods; but it may well be doubted if there has been any increase even of material happiness. Happiness is not in proportion to what one is able to consume, as our political economists would lead one to suppose, but in proportion of the supply to one's actual wants. We, with our present wants and habits, would be perfectly miserable for a time, if thrown back into the condition of the people of the middle ages; and yet it is probable they were better able to satisfy even such material or animal wants as were developed in them than we are to satisfy those developed in us. Human happiness is not augmented by multiplying human wants, without diminishing the proportion between them and the means of satisfaction, and that proportion has not been diminished, and cannot be, because such is human nature, that men's wants multiply always in even a greater ratio than the means of meeting them, as affirmed by our political economists, in their maxims of trade and production, that demand creates a supply, and supply creates a demand. Under the purely material relation, as a human animal, there is no doubt that the negro slave, well fed and well clothed, and not unkindly treated, is happier than the free laborer at wages. We suspect that it would be difficult to find in the world's history any age, in which the means of supply were less in proportion to the wants actually developed than in our own. There was more wisdom than our liberals are disposed to admit in the old maxim: If you would make a man happy, study not to augment his goods; but to diminish his wants. One of the greatest services Christianity has rendered the world has been its consecration of poverty, and its elevation of labor to the dignity of a moral duty. The tendency of modern society is in the opposite direction. England and the United States, the most modern of all modern nations, and the best exponents the world has of the tendencies of modern civilization, treat poverty as a crime, and hold honest labor should be endured by none who can escape it.

There is no question that education has been more generally diffused than it was in the middle ages, but it is doubtful if the number of thinkers has been increased, or real mental culture extended. Education loses in thoroughness and depth what it gains in surface. Modern investigators have explored nature to a greater extent than it appears to have ever been done by the ancients, and accumulated a mass of facts, or materials of science, at which many heads are turned; but little progress has been made in their really scientific classification and explanation. Theories and hypotheses in any number we have, each one of which is held by the simpletons of the age to be a real contribution to science when it is first put forth, but most of them are no better than soap-bubbles, and break and disappear as soon as touched. Christianity has taught the world to place a high estimate on the dignity of human nature, and has developed noble and humane sentiments, but under the progress of modern society in losing it, characters have been enfeebled and debased, and we find no longer the marked individuality, the personal energy, the manliness, the force, the nobility of thought and purpose, and the high sense of honor, so common in the mediæval world, and the better periods of antiquity. There is in our characters a littleness, a narrowness, a meanness, coupled with an astuteness and unscrupulousness to be matched only in the later stages of the Lower Empire. In military matters we have introduced changes, but may still study with advantage the Grecian phalanx and the Roman legion. Ulpian and Papinian can still, save in what we have learned from Christianity, teach us law, and we improve modern legislation and jurisprudence only by borrowing from the civil law as digested by the lawyers of Justinian, in the *Institutes* and *Novelloe*. In political science, properly so called, Aristotle, and any of the great mediæval doctors, are still competent to be our masters. He who has read Aristotle's *Politics* has read the history of American democracy, and the unanswerable refutation of all the democratic theories and tendencies of modern liberals. For the most part we are prone to regard what is new to us as new to the world, and, what is worse, what is new to us as a real scientific acquisition, and a real progress of the race.

We have never read or heard of any age that had so high an opinion of its own acquisitions, that believed so firmly in its own intelligence, and that so little questioned its own immense superiority over all preceding ages, as the eighteenth century. It believed itself enlightened, highly cultivated, profound, philosophic, humane, and yet the doctrines and theories that it placed in vogue, and over which the upper classes grew enthusiastic in their admiration, are so narrow, so shallow, so directly in the face and eyes of common sense, so manifestly false and absurd, that one finds it difficult to believe that anybody out of a madhouse ever entertained them. What think you of a philosopher who defines man—"A digesting tube, open at both ends"? and of another who ascribes all the difference between a man and a horse, for instance, to "the fact that man's fore limbs terminate in hands and flexible fingers, while those of a horse terminate in hoofs"? Yet these philosophers were highly esteemed in their day, and gave a tone to public opinion. We laugh at them as they did with the disciples of Epicurus, at the superstitions of past ages, the belief in sorcery, magic, necromancy, demons, witches, wizards, magicians, and yet all these things flourished in the eighteenth century, are believed in this nineteenth century in our own country, in England, France, and Germany, by men of all professions, and in all ranks of society. Wherein, then, consists the progress of our enlightment?

But "we are more liberal, more tolerant in matters of opinion, and have ceased to persecute men for religious differences," says our author. Hardly; yet if so, it may as well be because we are more indifferent, and less in earnest than our predecessors, believe less in mind, and more in matter. We have read no public documents more truly liberal and more tolerant in its spirit and provisions than the edict of Constantine the Great, giving liberty to Christians, and not taking it from pagans. Even Julian the Apostate professed as much liberality and tolerance as Voltaire, or Mazzini, and practised them as well as the liberals in Europe usually do, when in power. "But the age tends," replies our author, "to democracy, and, therefore, to the amelioration, and social and political elevation of the people." Fine words; but, in fact, while demagogues spout democracy, and modern literature sneers at law, mocks at loyalty, and preaches insubordination, insurrection, revolution, governments have a fine pretext for tightening their bonds, and rendering their power despotic; nay, in some respects, are compelled to do so, as the only means left of preventing the total dissolution of society and the lapse of the race into complete barbarism. If the system of repression is carried too far and threatens its own defeat, the exaggerations of liberalism provoke, and in part justify it, for the liberalistic tendencies, if unchecked, could lead only to anarchy. Democracy, understood not as a form of government, but as the end government is to seek, to wit, the common good, the advance in civilization of the people, the poorer and more numerous, as well as the richer and less numerous classes, not of a privileged caste or class, is a good thing, and a tendency towards it is really an evidence of social progress. But this is only what the great doctors of the church have always taught, when they have defined the end of government to be the good of the community, the public good, or the common good of all,—not the special good of a few, nor yet the greatest good of the greatest number, as taught by that grave and elaborate humbug, Jeremy Bentham, but the common good of all, that good which is common to all the members of the community, whether great or small, rich or poor.

But that democracy as the form of the government is the best practicable means of securing this end, unless restrained by constitutions, the most earnest and enlightened faith, and by the most pure and rigid religious discipline, is, to say the least, a perfectly gratuitous assumption. We defend here and everywhere, now and always, the political order established in our own country, and our failure—for failed, substantially, we have—is owing solely to our lack of real Christian faith, of the Christian conscience, and to our revolutionary attempts to interpret that order by the democratic theory. Our political order is republican, not democratic. But, in point of fact, the liberals have never advocated democracy for the end we have stated, from love of liberty, or for sake of ameliorating the condition of the people, though they may have so pretended, and at times even so believed, but really as a means of elevating themselves to power. Their democracy is, practically,—I am as good as you, and you have no more right than I to be in power or place. We believe in the disinterestedness or the patriotism of no man who can conspire to overthrow the government of his country, and whenever we hear a man professing great love for the dear people, praising their wisdom and virtue, their intelligence and sagacity, and telling them that they are sovereign, and their will ought to prevail, we always regard him as a self-seeker, and as desirous of using the people simply to elevate himself to be one of their rulers. Democracy elevates to places of honor, profit, and trust, men who could not be so elevated under any other form of government; but that this operates to the advantage of the public we have yet to learn.

What our author praises as the tendency of democracy, is the tendency to reduce all things to a low average, and to substitute popular opinion for truth, justice, reason, as the rule of action, and the criterion even of moral judgment. Democracy, when social as well as political, elevates not the best men to office, but the most available men, usually the most cunning, c r a f t y, or empty-headed demagogues. When, two years ago, the editor of this *Review* received the nomination in his district for member of congress, he was interiorly alarmed, and began a self-examination to ascertain what political folly or iniquity he had committed; and he became reconciled to himself, and his conscience was at ease, only when he found his election defeated by an overwhelming majority. His own defeat consoled him for his nomination, and restored his confidence in his own

integrity, loyalty, and patriotism. The men democracy usually elevates are petty attorneys or small
lawyers, men of large selfishness and small capacity,
and less political knowledge. The southern states,
whose democracy is less socially diffused than that
of the northern states, has always as a rule elevated
abler men than has the North, which has given them
an ascendency in the Union that has provoked northern jealousy. They have selected to represent them
in congress, in diplomacy, in the cabinet, in the presidential chair, their ablest men while we have selected
our feeblest men; or, if abler men, we have, with
rare exception, "rotated" them from their places
before they could acquire experience enough to be
useful. Democracy, in the sense we are considering
it, has shown what men it selects, when left to itself,
in the present administration, and in the last and
present congresses. Were there no better men in
the country? Then is democracy condemned, as
tending to degrade intellect and abase character, for
greater and better men we certainly had, who were
formed while we were yet British colonies. If there
were greater or better men, and democracy passed
them over as unavailable, then it is incapable of employing the best talent and the highest character produced by the country in its service, and therefore
should also be condemned. President Lincoln we
need not speak of; we have elsewhere given his
character. But we have not had a single statesman,
worthy of the name, in his cabinet or in congress
since the incoming of the present administration, and
hardly one from the free states since the Whigs, in
1840, descended into the forum, took the people by

the hand, and, led on by the *Boston Atlas* and the *New York Tribune,* undertook to be more democratic than the Democratic party itself, and succeeded in out-heroding Herod. When they dropped the name *Whig,* and assumed that of *Republican,* which we had recommended in place of *Democratic,* we, in our simplicity, supposed that they really intended to abandon Jacobinism and to contend for constitutionalism, else had we never for a moment supported them. But they did, and intended to do nothing of the sort.

There is nothing in the American experiment thus far to justify the liberals in identifying the progress of liberty and social well-being with the progress of democracy. On this point our author is wholly at fault. Since Mr. Van Buren, more incompetent men in the presidential chair we could not have had, if we had depended on the hereditary principle, than popular election has given us. Prince John [Van Buren] would have been better than Harrison or Taylor, and Prince Bob [Lincoln] can hardly fall below his father. We want no hereditary executive, but probably the chances of getting a wise man for president, if the executive were hereditary, would be greater than they have been under the elective principle, as our elections have been, for a long time, conducted. Seldom has our senate been equal to the English house of peers. Democracy opens a door to office to men who, under no other system, could ever attain to office; but their attainment to office is of no conceivable advantage to the public, and very little to themselves. It opens a door to every man's ambition, at least permits every man to indulge ambitious aspirations. When such a man as Abraham Lincoln can become president, who may not hope one day also to be president? It stimulates every one's ambition, every one's hope of office, perhaps of the highest in the gift of the people, but it does not stimulate any one to study or to labor to qualify himself for honorably discharging the duties of office. It is rare to find any man who does not think himself qualified for any office to which the people can be induced to elect him. The plurality of votes is a sovereign indorsement of his qualification. The people, in electing me, have judged me qualified, and would you, proud aristocrat, arraign the judgment of the people? Enough said.

The same tendency to democracy, lauded by our author, leads in nearly every thing, every one to struggle to be other than he is, to get what he has not, and to fill another place than the one he is in, and hence produces universal competition, and general uneasiness and discontent in society. No man is contented to live and die in the social position in which he was born, and pride and vanity, not love and humility, become the principle of all individual and social action. I am as good as Abraham Lincoln, and why should he be president and not I? He was a rail-splitter and I am a hod-carrier. Let me throw down the hod, as he did the beetle and wedge, become an attorney, and I may one day be president as well as he. John Jacob Astor was once a poor German boy, who landed alone and friendless in the streets of New York, and he died worth, some say, twenty-five millions, all made by himself in trade; and why not I do as much, and make as much money

as he? So every boy is discontented to remain at
home and follow the occupation of his father, that
of a mechanic or small farmer, and becomes anxious
to get a place in a counting-house, and to engage in
trade and speculation. Where all are free to aim to
be first no one is contented to be second, especially
to be last. This is the effect of liberalism, and an
effect which our author cites as an evidence of its
merit. He dwells on it with enthusiasm, and con-
trasts the movement, the activity, the aspirations of
the common people at present with that of the lower
classes under feudalism, and even the monarchical
régime of the sixteenth and seventeenth centuries.

We, although a true-born Yankee, think very dif-
ferently. Liberalism, taken in its practical workings
in a society, with weak faith, a movable religion, and
no loyalty, tends to develop wants which it is impossible to satisfy, because the wants it develops all
demand their satisfaction from the material order.
In the moral, intellectual, and spiritual world, the
multiplication of wants is in itself not an evil, because the means of satisfaction are liberally supplied, and even the very craving for moral or spiritual
good,—what the Gospel calls "a hungering and
thirsting after righteousness," is itself a good, and
blessed are they that do so, for they shall be filled.
But the multiplication of wants which can be satisfied only with material or sensible goods, is not a
good, but an evil. Political equality and equality
before the law is practicable, but social equality,
equality of wealth and social condition, is impracticable, and even undesirable. Only one man, once in
four years, out of many millions, can be president of

the United States; and if all set their hearts on it, all but the one must be disappointed. The sufferings of disappointed office-seekers more than overbalance the pleasures of office-holders. All cannot be rich, for if all were rich, paradoxical as it may sound, all would be poor. Real wealth is not in the magnitude of one's possessions, but in the amount of the labor of others one is able to command; and if all are rich, no one can command any labor of another at all, for there is no one to sell his labor, and the rich man is reduced precisely to the level of the poor man. Though his possessions are counted by millions, he must produce for himself, and actually have only what he can produce with the labor of his own hands. All your schemes of an equal division of property, and for keeping all the members of a community equal in their condition, are fallacious, and, if they could be carried out, would end only in establishing universal poverty, universal ignorance, and universal barbarism. The human race would soon sink everywhere below the condition of our North American savages and, indeed, liberalism is practically a tendency to the savage state, as any one may learn even from Jean Jacques Rousseau.

We want no privileged caste or class; we want no political aristocracy, recognized and sustained as such by law. Let all be equal before the law. But we do want a social aristocracy, families elevated by their estates, their public services, their education, culture, manners, tastes, refinement, above the commonalty; and we do not believe a community can long even subsist where such an aristocracy is wanting, to furnish models and leaders for the people.

It is the presence of such an aristocracy, that in the present fearful struggle gives to the southern states their unity and strength. It is the want of such a class, enjoying the confidence and respect of the people in the loyal states, that constitutes our national weakness, as we have elsewhere shown. The people, we have said, and we all know, must have leaders and leaders must be born, not made. The number in a nation who have the qualities to be leaders, whether in peace or war, are comparatively few. All cannot lead; the mass must follow, and those who are born to follow should be content to follow, and not aspire to lead. If you stir up in them the ambition to lead, make them discontented with their lot, and determined to pass from followers to leaders, you reverse the natural order of things, introduce confusion into society, disorder into all ranks, and do good to nobody. We ourselves, we know it well, were never born to lead, and should only be misplaced, and ruin ourselves and others, were we put in the position of a leader. Our author professes to be a philosopher, and to have mastered what just now is called the science of sociology,—a barbarous term, which we detest,—and therefore he ought to understand that he is calling things by wrong names; that practically he says, Evil be thou my good! and, if successful, would erect a pandæmonium, not a well ordered human society, or a temple of liberty and peace.

Yet our author swims with the current, and is sustained by all the force of what is regarded as the advanced opinion of the age, and for the moment is stronger than we, who are sustained only by certain

moral instincts and traditions which are generally un-
heeded. He has, too, the ear of the public, if not
for himself personally, yet for innumerable others
who agree with him, and can speak with even far
more force and eloquence than he; while we are re-
pudiated by all parties, by all sects, and only a few
will listen to or heed our voice, harsh and discordant
as it is in most ears. We are neither an *obscurantist*
nor a liberal, but agreeing in some things, and
disagreeing in others, with both; precisely the sort
of a man, no party likes, for we can support no
party through thick and thin,—a legitimate child of
the nineteenth century, yet believing that all wisdom
was neither born nor will die with it. We believe
there were "brave men before Agamemnon," and
that there will be brave men even after we are dead
and forgotten. We belong not to the party that
would restore the past, but to that which would
retain what was true and good, and for all ages, in
the past; we are not of those who would destroy
the past, and compel the human race to begin *de
novo,* but of those, few in number they may be, who
see something good even in liberalism, and would
accept it without breaking the chain of tradition, or
severing the continuity of the life of the race, separate it from the errors and falsehoods, and bitter and
hateful passions with which it is mixed up, and carry
it onward. We are too much of the present to please
the men of the past, and too much of the past to
please the men of the present; so we are not only
doomed, Cassandra-like, to utter prophecies which
nobody believes, but prophecies which nobody heeds
either to believe or disbelieve. We know it well, and

therefore we said, We were not born to be a leader, although we have been long since spoiled as a follower, like most of our contemporaries. Hence, though we know that we speak the words of truth and soberness, we expect not our words to be heeded. Popular opinion decides with us all questions of wisdom and folly, of truth and falsehood, and popular opinion we do not and cannot echo.

Our author is a liberal, and ultra-democrat, a revolutionist,—has been, and probably still is, a conspirator,—a man who sees no sacredness in law, no inviolability in authority, and no charm in loyalty. His political creed is short, and very precise. It is: "The people are sovereign; the people are divine; the people are infallible and impeccable; I and my fellow-conspirators and revolutionists are the people; and because you Americans will not permit us to assume the direction of your civil and military affairs, you are no true liberals, no consistent democrats, and are really hostile to the progressive tendencies of the modern world." This is his creed, and the creed of all such as he, whether at home or abroad. We do not believe his creed, and have no wish to see it prevail. Many Americans profess it: few of them, however, really believe it, or, in fact, much else. They have been in the habit of hearing it, of reading it in newspapers and novels, and listening to it from the lips of impassioned orators on the Fourth of July, and in political meetings, and they have repeated it, as a matter of course, without giving it one moment's serious thought; but their instincts are truer than the creed they now and then fancy they believe, and there still linger in their minds faint reminiscences of something better, which was once believed by most men, and approved by Christian faith and conscience.

If the American people could only once understand that the present war is not a war between democracy and aristocracy, but a war in defence of government and law, that is, in defence of authority in principle as well as in practice, against popular license and revolutionism, the war, however it might terminate, would prove the richest boon they have ever as a people received from the hand of Heaven. It would arrest that lawless and revolutionary tendency they have hitherto thoughtlessly followed, which they have fancied it belonged to them to encourage both at home and abroad, and which at times has threatened to make us the pest of the civilized world. We trust it will yet have this effect. We are radical, if you will, in our determination, at the earliest moment it can be legally done, to get rid of the system of slave-labor, but, thank God, a radical in nothing else, and sympathize in little else with those who are called radicals: and, after all, we suspect the mass of the American people agree more nearly with us than with our General Croaker, and that we are a truer exponent of their real interior convictions and social instincts than he, although they will never believe it because they will never read us; and the journals, if they notice us at all, will only misrepresent and pervert our words. Yet we rely greatly on military discipline and the effects of the war, to bring back the people to sounder political and social views.

CHAPTER FIVE

THE DEMOCRATIC PRINCIPLE

NOTE ON "THE DEMOCRATIC PRINCIPLE"

A tireless old man, Brownson published in his *Quarterly Review* for April, 1873, this brief essay which summarizes admirably the whole of his political philosophy. True constitutions—as he had written so often—are the work of Providence, operating through the historical experience of the several nations; and if the paper constitution of a state arbitrarily disavows the divine ordination of political authority, it is no real constitution at all. The American tendency to give their constitution a democratic interpretation is a sorry corruption of old republican institutions. Modern democracy, enamored of Bentham, endeavors to set up a mundane conventional sanction for constitutions, disowning the religious origins of justice. Feeling itself emancipated from moral restraints, democracy gives over a people to avarice and intolerance. "We thus, under our democratic system, pay a premium for dishonesty, cheatery, and knavery, and then are astonished at the daily increase of fraud and crime in the business world." The gospel of "free competition", as a substitute for religious veneration, corrupts society quite as thoroughly as communism would. "This is what our age calls liberty, what it means by liberty of conscience, that is, getting rid of all laws that bind the national conscience, and thus severing politics from the moral order, and subjecting the moral order itself to the secular authority, however constituted." Like so many of Brownson's essays, this article has grown in meaning with the passage of the decades.

*   *   *

[From *Brownson's Quarterly Review* for April, 1873.]

During our late civil war it was almost proverbial to call our government the best government under heaven; and whoever in the loyal states expressed an opinion to the contrary ran some risk of being sent to Fort Lafayette, Fort Warren, or to some other federal place of imprisonment. I defended the government during those fearful times, and stood by it when many a stout heart failed, because it was the government of *my* country, and I owed it the allegiance due from the citizen; but never since the "Hard-Cider" campaign have I believed it practically "the best government under heaven," or superior to almost any other civilized government. "Tippecanoe and Tyler too" upset my democracy, by showing how easily the people can be humbugged and carried away by a song. Till then I had believed in democracy, though I believed in little else.

My friend, George Bancroft, defined democracy, in a lecture which I published in my *Boston Quarterly Review,* to be "eternal justice ruling through the people:" I defined it in a series of resolutions adopted by a Democratic state convention, to be the "supremacy of man over his accidents"—meaning thereby that democracy regards the man as more than his possessions, social position, or any thing separable from his manhood—and got most unmercifully ridiculed for it; but the ridicule did not move me, and I held fast to the doctrine, that the will of the people is the most direct and authentic expression of the divine will that can be had or desired. The people held with me then, in some respects, the place the church now holds with me. I labored under the comfortable illusion that, in order to secure wise and just government, all I had to do was to remove all restrictions on the free and full expression of the popular will, and to leave the people free to follow in all things their own divine instincts. The defects of bad legislation to which I could not shut my eyes, I attributed not to democracy, but to the fact that the democratic principle was obstructed, and the will of the people could not have its free and full expression. There were still many restraints on their will, retained from old monarchical and aristocratic institutions; such as an independent judiciary, and the English common law with its subtilties and technicalities. These should all be swept away, and the unrestrained will of the people be supreme, and make itself felt alike in the administration of justice, and the election of representatives in the legislature and in all the offices of the government, state or national. To secure the rule of justice and the recognition of the man over his accidents, every thing should be swept away that imposed the least check on the direct and immediate action of the popular will. People, though adopting the democratic principle, told me I went too far, but I knew I was logical; and I have never in my life been able to persuade myself that a principle, really sound and true, will not bear pushing to its last logical consequences. If the democratic principle will not bear being so pushed, it is simply a proof that it is untrue, and cannot be safely adopted. This was my reasoning then, and is my reasoning now. The country, public opinion, gave me the principle, furnished me the democratic premises, and I took it for granted that the principle was sound and the premises indisputable, as do the majority of my countrymen.

The "Hard-Cider" campaign of 1840 came. In it I took an active part on the Democratic side, in behalf of Martin Van Buren, the last first-class man that sat, or probably that ever will sit, in the presidential chair of the United States; and my party was, as all the world knows, woefully defeated. It was the first presidential campaign in which I had ever taken an active part, and almost my first experience in practical politics. It was enough. What I saw served to dispel my democratic illusions, to break the idol I had worshipped, and shook to its foundation my belief in the divinity of the people, or in their will as the expression of eternal justice. I saw that they could be easily duped, easily made victims of the designing, and carried away by an irresistible passion in the wrong as easily as in the right. I was forced by the shock my convictions received, to review first my logic, and then to examine the premises which I had taken on trust from my democratic countrymen which I had not hitherto thought of questioning. I found them untenable and absurd. I ceased henceforth to believe in democracy, but I did not cease to be a loyal citizen, nor did I deem it necessary to abandon the Democratic party so called, which after all, was less unsound, less radical, and more conservative than the Whig party, which had carried the elections; but I labored day and night with voice and pen, in the *Boston Quarterly Review* and in the *Democratic Review,* to make it still more conservative, and to convince its leaders that the people as the state need governing no less than the people as individuals. So I labored till my happy conversion to the church, when, having no associations with the Catholic population of the country, except our common Catholic faith, I ceased to have any political influence; and if I resume the discussion of political topics, it is solely with the hope of being of some service to my ingenuous, pure-minded, and educated young Catholic friends, destined to exert a powerful influence for good or for evil on the political future of the republic.

The great democratic principle was asserted by the congress of 1776, in the declaration that "Governments derive their just powers from the assent of the governed." They thus declared that governments originate in convention, and that law derives its force as law from the will of those it is to bind. This asserts the purely human origin of government, and rejects all law enjoined by any authority above the people. It denies the right or authority of any government to command, for no such right or authority can be created by any convention or agreement; it denies, also, all law that restrains the will of the governed. That the law binds only by virtue of the assent of those on whom it is to operate, Gallicans asserted in principle, in asserting that papal constitutions do not bind the conscience unless assented to, at least tacitly, by the church. This principle, which reverses all one's natural ideas of government and law, the recent Council of the Vatican has condemned, when applied in the spiritual or ecclesiastical order; and we see no reason why a Catholic should not condemn it, when applied in the political and civil order. No government that has real authority to govern, can originate in convention alone; for the convention itself needs to be authorized by a law or an authority superior to itself, since St. Paul teaches, *Non est potestas nisi a Deo*. Where there is no law of nations, which the nation itself is bound to obey, there may be national force, but no national right or authority to govern. Laws that emanate from the people, or that are binding only by virtue of the assent of the governed, or that emanate from any human source alone, have none of the essential characteristics of law, for they bind no conscience, and restrain, except by force, no will.

We do not allege that human governments have no legislative authority or power to enact laws and bind the conscience; but that authority, that power is not derived from a human source, and is held only by the divine law under which they are constituted. Governments that have only a conventional origin, and only such powers as are held from the assent of the governed, have no such authority, no such power. The grand objection to democracy, then, is, that it rejects the law of nations, the *jus gentium*, denies the rule of eternal and immutable right, and resolves eternal justice into mere conventionalism, and, if a government at all, it is simply a government of force, under which might makes right. I am not arguing against a republic, or a government largely popular in its constitution and administration, such as ours was intended to be; but against the democratic principle, that founds government in convention, and derives it powers from the consent of the governed, or which applies to the civil order the Gallican principle, condemned by the Council of the Vatican, when applied in the spiritual or ecclesiastical order. It makes the people who are to be governed superior to the government, and leaves their will supreme, subject to no authority, bound by no law. It is, therefore, simply the principle of political atheism. So far as the national authority is concerned, the principle is not confined to a popularly constituted government, but is accepted and acted on by most modern governments, especially by the Sardinian, the Prussian, the Russian, and we fear also the Austrian, in none of which is the law of nations, binding the conscience of the nation itself, recognized.

The American constitution is not founded on political atheism, but recognizes the rights of man, and, therefore, the rights of God. There remain as yet among us some traces of the law of nations, in distinction from the international law of Benthamites and diplomates, which consists solely in conventional pacts and precedents, without any recognition of the rule of right, or of eternal and immutable justice. Something of Christian tradition lives among us and is kept alive by the common law and the judicial department of the government, though, latterly, too often overruled by the legislative department which is continually encroaching on the province of the judiciary, as we see in much recent congressional legislation. What we complain of is the tendency of American public opinion, formed and directed to a great extent by popular journalism, to apply the naked, unmitigated democratic principle to the interpretation of the constitution and what we call our American institutions; though what is really meant by this phrase which is in every one's mouth, it would be hard to say. Public opinion with us asserts and applies the democratic principle, which, as we have seen, liberates the people as the state from all government, and their will from all restraint; and leaves them perfectly untrammelled, free to do whatever they have the physical force to do. Their might founds and measures their right.

Is it not so? If not, why are the public so sensitive to the assertion of any authority above the people, or of a law which does not emanate from the people and which they are bound in conscience, collectively as well as individually, to obey? Why does our American public opinion applaud Prince Bismarck and Victor Emanuel for their efforts to subject all authorities or powers in the nation to the national government. In this country our Protestant fellow-citizens, being the majority, take great credit to themselves for "tolerating," as Dr. Bellows puts it, the Catholic faith and worship. Why, if not because they hold themselves free to prohibit them, if they should choose? Are they not, in fact, using the power numbers give them, to invade the Catholic conscience and deprive Catholics of their equal rights as parents and citizens, by compelling them to pay for the support of schools to which they are forbidden by conscience to send their children? Evidently they recognize no law of right or justice to which their will is subject, and which we may plead as our protection. The plea of justice in regard to public measures is rarely heard. Utility or expediency, not right or justice, is the standard adopted in politics, as external decorum or propriety is the rule in ethics. Even the late William H. Seward, when he appealed from the constitution of the United States, which as senator he had sworn to observe, to the "higher law," only appealed from one human law to another, or from the particular to the general; for he appealed only to general humanity, whose rights he never dreamed of identifying with the rights of God. If the abolition party he represented appealed to the law of God as the law of nations, it was to that law without any court or tribunal to declare and apply it, and as interpreted and applied by the party itself. The abolitionist, with all his fine talk, fierce declamation in favor of a law above the state, would have recoiled from the assertion of a divinely instituted court or tribunal to interpret it and give it practical efficacy in the government of men and nations. He asserted it, but only on the condition that he should be free to interpret and apply it for himself; and hence his individualism nullified the law, and his humanitarianism was resolved, sometimes even avowedly, into no-governmentism.

I repeat, I am not warring against the political constitution of my country, nor am I seeking in any respect to change it; for I am no revolutionist, no monarchist, no aristocrat. It is the spirit and opinions of the American people, or of the majority of them, that I want changed, and so changed as to interpret the constitution of American political society by the principles of law and justice, not by the democratic principle, which asserts the sovereignty of the arbitrary will of the people, or, practically, the unrestricted rule of the majority for the time: which is tyranny, and repugnant to the very essence of liberty, which is will ruled by right, or power controlled by justice.

The philosophers and statesmen of the last century supposed that the evil could be prevented, and the necessary restraints on the popular will or ruling majority could be imposed, by means of written constitutions, which, in the words of the Thetford stay-maker, author of the *Age of Reason,* could be "folded up and filed away in a pigeon-hole." They supposed the people emancipated from superstition, as they called religion, and from priests and priest-craft, and left to the promptings of their simple nature, would always be guided by reason, and therefore needed only to be governed in their action by a wise and just written constitution. They held the people could be safely entrusted with the guardianship of the constitution, which was very much like locking up a man in prison, and giving him the key. But experience has proved that written constitutions, unless they are written in the sentiments, convictions, consciences, manners, customs, habits, and organization of the people, are no better than so much waste paper, and can no more restrain them than the green withes with which the Philistines bound his limbs, could restrain the mighty Samson.

John C. Calhoun, the most sagacious and accomplished statesman our republic has ever produced, and who appreciated the tyranny of majorities better than any other man amongst us, placed no confidence in written constitutions; but he hoped to restrain the popular will by dividing and organizing the people according to their different sectional pursuits and interests, or by organizing a system of "concurrent majorities." This would be, no doubt, an advance on simply written constitutions; but it is only in communities where the pursuits and interests of different sections of the population are very distinct, that it is practicable, or could be efficacious. Since the abolition of slavery, the population, pursuits, and interests of the whole country are too homogeneous to allow the organization he demanded, or to admit the system of concurrent majorities. If introduced, it would be rendered ineffective by the great homogeneous interests and pursuits of the majority of the population, which would overpower and trample on all minorities opposed to them.

We hold that whatever constitutional or organic provisions may be adopted, the stronger interest of a country, in the absence of all recognition of the law of nations, limiting and defining the rights and powers of the nation, will govern the country, whether the interest and pursuits of the numerical majority or not; or at least dictate the policy of its government. For a time the southern states could protect their interests, and, to some extent, shape the policy of the government, because they represented the strongest of any one interest of the country, the interest of capital invested in labor; but when short crops and wars in Europe had created a demand for our breadstuffs and provisions, the products of the non-slaveholding states, and the produce of the California mines had strengthened the commercial and manufacturing interests, which already controlled the free states, and enabled the representatives of these interests to meet their foreign exchanges,—they were stronger than any interests the South could oppose to them. The South had then no alternative, but either to submit to be controlled by them, as the people of the non-slaveholding states were, or to secede from the Union, and endeavor to establish an independent republic for themselves. The struggle was a struggle of interests. The abolition fanatics were only the fly on the wheel, and the question they raised amounted to nothing in itself, and was of importance only as it was seized upon as a pretext, and had only this significance, that the business interests of the North could subject the interests of the South to their control only by destroying the southern capital invested in labor. Mr. Calhoun's policy, if carried out, might have staved off the crisis for a few years, but could not have prevented it or its final results.

I have said, in the absence of the law of nations, which, it cannot be too often repeated, is law for the nation, as well as for the individual, therefore law emanating from an authority above the nation, above and over the people. The attempt of modern statesmen, Mr. Calhoun among the rest, to constitute the state without any power or authority above the people, so that by its own spontaneous working it should maintain order with liberty, and liberty with order, promote the highest utility and the greatest happiness of the nation, is a vain attempt. The thing is impossible. No simply human wisdom, no adjustment of positive and negative forces, no organization of interests, or system of checks and balances, will do it. The English in their constitution have carried to perfection their system of checks and balances, or of the organization of separate interests, classes, or estates, each with a negative on the others; yet, in spite of the national boasts, it works with difficulty, and one of the separately organized estates is swallowing up the others. It, in its present form, is hardly a century and a half old, and it undergoes a greater or less change every few years. The prosperity of England under it is commercial and industrial, and is due less to it, than to the fact that she has invented the art of converting debt into capital; and by means of the revolutions, and the wars growing out of them, of the continental states, she has contrived to bring the nations of the Old World and the New into debt to her, and to compel them to pour their surplus earnings into her lap. The nations live and labor to enrich her; and yet her overgrown wealth consists chiefly in paper evidences of credit, and might vanish in a day. Then her wealth is unequally distributed: a few are very rich in paper values, but in no country on earth is there greater poverty or more squalid wretchedness. Then we must take into the account her government of Ireland and India, worse than any of the pro-consular governments of ancient Rome. She, also, owes more to her mines of tin, lead, iron, and coal, soon to be exhausted, than to the excellence of her political constitution, or the wisdom of her statesmen.

I cannot conceive a more profoundly philosophic, or more admirably devised constitution, than that of our own government, as I have endeavored truthfully to present it in my *American Republic*. Yet, for the lack of the moral element in the American people, for the lack of a recognition of the law of nations emanating from an authority above the people, and binding the conscience of the nation, it is practically disregarded, and its wisest and most vital provisions are treated by the ruling people as *non avenues*. The people have forgotten its providential origin, treat it as their own creature, as a thing they have made, and may alter or unmake at their pleasure. It is not a law enjoined on them, and has no hold on their conscience. They give it a purely democratic interpretation. Men talk of loyalty, but men cannot be loyal to what is below them and dependent on their breath; and, therefore, they violate it without compunction, as often as prompted to do so by their interests or their passions. Nothing was more striking during the late civil war than the very general absence of loyalty or feeling of duty, on the part of the adherents of the Union, to support the government because it was the legal government of the country, and every citizen owed it the sacrifice of his life, if needed. The administration never dared confide in the loyalty of the federal people. The appeals made were to interest, to the democracy of the North against the aristocracy of the South; to anti-slavery fanaticism, or to the value and utility of the Union, rarely to the obligation in conscience to support the legitimate or legal authority; prominent civilians were bribed by high military commissions; others, by advantageous contracts for themselves or their friends for supplies to the army;

and the rank and file, by large bounties and high wages. There were exceptions, but such was the rule.

"I will have a draft," said the secretary of war, Mr. Stanton, to me one day in his office: "I will have a draft, if I get but one man by it, for I wish to assert the majesty of this government, its right to command the support of citizens in the ranks of the army, or elsewhere, in its hour of need. This reliance on large bounties and high wages, that is running up an enormous bill of expenses which the people must ultimately pay, is derogatory to the majesty of the government, obscures and weakens its authority, and appeals only to the lowest and most sordid motives of the human heart."—Well, the draft was ordered, and, as we all know, proved a failure. The government, indeed, asserted its majesty, but the people did not recognize it; they effectively resisted it, or came to a compromise. How could they see a majesty in a government they themselves had made and could unmake? The universal conviction of the conventional origin of the government despoiled it of its majesty. It had no majesty, no authority, but what it held from the people, and could command no obedience but such as they chose to give it. If it went further, it was by force, not by right: and fully did the administration feel it.

The conventional origin of the constitution excludes its moral or divine right, and therefore denies all obligation in conscience of the people, either collectively or individually, to obey it. It has nothing in it that one is morally bound to treat as sacred and inviolable. Its violation is no moral offence, for it is the violation of no moral law, of no eternal and immutable right. Nothing hinders the people, when they find the constitution in the way of some favorite project on which they are bent, from trampling it under their feet, and passing on as if it never had any existence. The constitution, to be respected, must be clothed with a moral authority, an authority for conscience, which it cannot be, if of conventional origin; and the government constituted has no just powers not derived from the assent of the governed.

This is wherefore no constitutional contrivances or combinations, however artistic or skilful, can be successful that have no support in the divine order. The government which has no authority for conscience—and none that holds not from God, and under his law, has or can have any authority for conscience—having no moral support, is impotent to govern, except by sheer force, as we have already shown over and over again. Now, as the modern statesmen exclude the moral order, and make no account of the divine element in society, and rely on the human element alone, they are unable to clothe power with right, or to give it any stability. The revolutionary spirit is everywhere at work, and is kept down and a semblance of order maintained in Europe only by five millions of armed soldiers. In our own country, we owe such orders as we have, first, to the fact that the government acts less as a government, than as a factor or agent of the controlling, that is, the business interests of the country; and second, to the fact that the American people are not yet completely democratized, but retain, in spite of their theory of the conventional origin of power, no little of their traditionary respect for authority, and their obligation in conscience to obey the law. Yet, under the influence of their democratic training, they are fast losing what they have thus far retained from an epoch prior to the rejection of the divine order by statesmen and the constitutions of states.

Democracy which asserts the conventional origin of government, and thus excludes the divine order from the state, necessarily denies with Jeremy Bentham all rules of right, eternal and immutable, and can at best assert only the rule of utility, or, as commonly expressed, "the greatest happiness of the greatest number''; though Bentham himself changed in his later days the formula, and, for the greatest happiness of the greatest number, substituted as his political, juridical, and ethical formula, simply "the greatest happiness." This is the only formula of the sort that the purely democratic principle can adopt or accept. Democrats tell us this end is to be gained by getting rid of the burden of kings and aristocrats, and introducing not only equality before the law, but equality of rights and privileges, and carrying out the great principle, "All men are created equal." Equality of privileges is an absurdity, and there can be no rights where there is no right. But pass over this. "Democracy asserts and maintains equality!" Yes, *asserts* it, we grant, but it tends to promote the contrary. It operates practically, almost exclusively, in favor of those who command and employ capital or credit in business, and against the poorer and more numerous classes.

The political equality, expressed by universal suffrage and eligibility, is of no practical value; for,
however elections may go, or whoever may be
elected, the legislation will invariably follow the
stronger interest, therefore the business interests of
the country: it may be now the commercial interests,
now the industrial or manufacturing interests, or,
in fine, the railroad, and other business corporation
interests. There is no help for it in universal suffrage.
By excluding the moral element and founding the
state on utility, democracy tends to materialize the
mind, and to create a passion for sensible goods, or
material wealth and well-being. Take any ten thousand electors at random, and ask them what they
want of government, and the honest answer will be:
"Such legislative action as will facilitate the acquisition of wealth." Suppose such action taken—and
most of our legislation is of that sort—how many of
the ten thousand are in a position to profit by it?
perhaps, ten; perhaps, not more than one. Democracy excludes aristocracy in the European sense,
an aristocracy founded on large landed estates, noble
birth, education, and manners; and substitutes for it
an aristocracy founded on business capacity and
capital or credit, a thousand times worse and more
offensive, because more exacting, more insolent and
haughty, always afraid of compromising its dignity
by mingling with the poor or unfashionable, feeling
that it is a sort of usurper, without any hereditary
or legitimate claims to respect,—an aristocracy of
roturiers, the most contemptible as well as, socially
and politically, the most galling of all possible aristocracies. We do not object to a man, or refuse to

honor him, because he has risen from the gutter; but we do refuse to honor a man who was born in a gutter and has remained there, but claims respect simply because he has succeeded in gathering a mass of gold around him.*

Democracy, following the lead of the business classes, builds up, and with us has covered the land over with huge business and moneyed corporations, which the government itself cannot control. We complain of the great feudal barons, that they were often more powerful than their suzerain; but our railroad "kings" can match the most powerful vassals, either of the king of France, or of the king of England, in feudal times. Louis XI was not weaker against Charles the Bold, than is congress against the Pennsylvania Central Railroad and its connections, or the Union Pacific, built at the expense of the government itself. The great feudal barons had souls, railroad corporations have none. Congress cannot resume specie payments, for the national-bank interest opposes it; and so our commercial

---

* There is no mistake in saying that the mass of the electoral people demand of government such legislation in relation to business interests, as will facilitate the acquisition of wealth; nor in saying that all legislation of the sort does and must, as far as it has any effect, favor inequality, and enrich the few at the expense of the many. If all could avail themselves equally of such legislation, nobody would or could derive any advantage from it, and it would facilitate the acquisition of wealth for no one. Where there has been bad legislation, legislation creating monopolies, or conferring special business privileges on individuals, or a particular class or corporation, the repeal by the government of such legislation, may have, to a certain extent, the effect demanded, by removing restrictions. But no other legislation, save such as secures the citizen an open field for exertion, and the full possession of the fruits of his honest industry for facilitating acquisition of wealth, is possible except by facilitating the transferrence of the earning of the many to the pockets of the few. Such is the effect of all laws designed to facilitate the operations of the business classes, and to promote business interests. Whether this is a good or an evil, certainly the inevitable tendency of universal suffrage and eligibility is to inequality, not to equality, as is pretended.

interests must bear the loss of a depreciated currency, and the laboring classes must continue to pay the higher prices for the necessaries of life it creates. In a word, the business classes, according to the old Whig party, the "urban party" of the time of Swift and Addison, or of Queen Anne's reign, have permanent possession of the government, and use it to further their own interests, which is a damage; for this country is fitted to be, and really is, a great agricultural country.

In the *Review* for January,* I showed the disastrous influence which the equality, asserted by democracy, and supposed to be favored by universal suffrage and eligibility, has on the laboring classes. It is to the honor of the church that she has always had a special regard and tenderness for the poor; and it is no less to her honor that she never attempted to remove poverty. She always relieves distress when able, and solaces suffering whatever its cause; but she honors the poor, and treats poverty as a blessing, not as a misfortune. In her view, the poor are really the more favored class, and she never attempts, and has never enjoined it upon her children to attempt, to place them, as to the goods of this world, on an equality with the rich. She holds the thing neither practicable nor desirable. Democracy regards the poor as unfortunate, and undertakes to remove poverty by opening to them all the avenues of wealth, and to elevate them by establishing their political and civil equality; and thus leads them, as we see in the recently enfranchised negroes, to aspire to social equality. This causes them to be discontented with

* See "The Political State of the Country."

their lot, and makes them feel their poverty a real misery. It greatly enhances the expenses of their living. As a rule, men live for their families, especially for their wives and daughters, whom they would see live as well, be as well educated, and as well dressed as the wives and daughters of the better-to-do, whom democracy teaches them to regard as equals. The evil this causes is immeasurable. It induces not a few to live beyond their means, or to make a show of wealth which they have not; it creates a universal struggle to escape poverty, and to acquire riches as a means of equality and respectability. The passion for wealth, so strong in most Americans, and which is called by foreigners "the worship of the almighty dollar," is at bottom only the desire to escape poverty and the disgrace attached to it by democracy. Political economists regard this struggle with favor, for it stimulates production and increases the wealth of the nation, which would be true enough, if consumption did not fully keep pace with production; though, if true, we could hardly see, in the increased wealth of the nation, a compensation for the private and domestic misery it causes, and the untold amount of crime of which it is the chief instigator. We regard it as an unmixed evil which could and would be avoided, if poverty were honored, and the honest and virtuous poor were respected according to their real worth, as they are by the church, and were in all old Catholic countries till the modern democratic spirit invaded them. "A contented mind is a continual feast," says the proverb.

Democracy, by its delusive universal suffrage and eligibility, stimulates a universal passion, as we have seen, for social equality, which can be gratified only by the possession of wealth or material goods; for democracy, excluding the moral order, can content no one with moral equality. "I am as good as you, and why should you be rich and I poor? Why should you live in a palace, and I in a mud hovel? Why should you ride in your coach and live in luxury, while I must trudge on foot, be thinly clad, and live on the coarsest and most meagre fare, which I can procure only with difficulty, sometimes not at all?"— Just consider that there are in the city of New York, at least, forty thousand children, orphans or worse than orphans, absolutely homeless, who live by begging and thieving, and lodge on doorsteps, under the wharves, and in miserable dens; initiated, almost as soon as able to speak, into every vice and crime that finds opportunity or shelter in a great city: contrast these with the children brought up in elegant and luxurious homes, bearing in mind that democracy asserts equality, and say, if there is any thing singular in the logic that concludes communism from democratic premises, or if a Wendell Phillips is not a true and consistent democrat in defending the Paris commune and the internationale? Or if, when you denounce either as infamous, you do not forget your democracy, and borrow from an order of ideas that, though approved by Christian tradition, democracy excludes, or at least makes no account of?

But communism, which demands equality in material goods, is not only an impossibility, but an absurdity. Equality of wealth is equivalent to equal-

ity of poverty. Wealth consists in its power to purchase labor, and no matter how great it is, it can
purchase no labor, if there is none in the market;
and, if all were equally rich, there would be none in
the market, for no one would sell his labor to another. Then each man would be reduced to what he
can produce with his own hands, wealth would lose
all the advantages it has where there are rich and
poor, and society would lapse after a generation or
two into the lowest barbarism. Communism, if it
could be carried out, would not, then, as the com-
munists dream, secure to all the advantages of
wealth, but would result in the reduction of all to the
most abject poverty,—the very thing which they are
ready to commit any crime or sacrilege in order to
escape. All projects of reform of any sort, under-
taken without divine authority and guidance, in-
evitably defeat themselves, and aggravate the evils
they would redress. Reject the communistic conclusion. The democratic equality asserted, then, can
be, practically, only free competition, making all
equally free to compete for wealth, and the good
things of this world, and leaving each free to possess
what he acquires. This is the interpretation democracy receives with us. But in this competition there
is only a delusive equality. In it the honest man
stands no chance with the dishonest. The baker who
feels bound to furnish thirty-two ounces in his two-
pound loaf, cannot compete with him who has no
scruple in charging the full price of a two-pound
loaf for eighteen ounces. So throughout the whole
business world. It would be undemocratic for the
law to interfere to protect those who are unable, no

matter from what cause, to protect themselves. The law must leave all things of the sort to free competition, and to regulate themselves. We thus, under our democratic system, pay a premium for dishonesty, cheatery, and knavery, and then are astonished at the daily increase of fraud and crime in the business world. We tempt men to get rich—honestly if they may, but at any rate to get rich—by the contempt in which we hold poverty, and the honor which we pay to wealth, as I have already intimated. Universal suffrage and eligibility can at best secure only this so-called free competition, and enact laws favorable to the acquisition of wealth. But men's natural capacities are unequal; and these laws, which on their face seem perfectly fair and equal, create monopolies which enrich a few individuals at the expense of the many. There is far less equality, as well as less honesty and integrity, in American society, than there was fifty or sixty years ago. The honor paid to wealth, or what is called success in the world, is greater; people are less contented with moderate means, a moderate style of living, as well as with moderate gains, and have a much greater horror of honest labor. I remember when it was, in the country at least, regarded as an act of prudence for a young couple with little or nothing but health, industrious habits, and a willingness to earn their living by hard work, to marry and set up housekeeping for themselves. Now, except to a very limited extent, it would be regarded as the greatest imprudence. No little of that remarkable purity and morality for which the Catholic peasantry of Ireland are noted the world over, is due to early marriages, which

the habits of the people encourage. Yet English and
American economists denounce them, and represent them as due to the craft of the clergy who encourage them for the sake of the wedding-fee, and of
the baptismal fee most likely in due time to follow.
The purity and morality of our New England people—I speak of them, for I was brought up among
them—have diminished in very nearly the same
ratio in which early marriages have been discon-
tinued as imprudent, except with the very rich. The
class of small farmers who cultivated their own
farms, and by their labor, economy, and frugality
obtained a comfortable living, and were able to
establish one son in business, and to educate another to be a lawyer, a doctor, or a minister, to
provide moderate portions for the daughters, and to
leave the homestead to the eldest son,—has dis-
appeared, and they have been obliged to emigrate, to
exile themselves from their early homes and all the
endearing associations of childhood and youth,
though they go not beyond the limits of their own
country. I myself am even more an exile in my present residence, than my Irish or German neighbor;
for he has near him those whom he was brought up
with, who knew him in his youth, while I have not
one,—not one with whom I can talk over old times,
or who knew me before I had reached middle age:
and my case has in it nothing peculiar. But the fact,
that no small portion of the American people have
been separated from the old homestead and scat-
tered among strangers, has a fatal influence in check-
ing the development of their finer qualities, and in

throwing them for relief upon the coarser passions and grosser pleasures of sense.

There is less equality than there was in my boyhood, and the extremes are greater. The rich are richer, and the poor are poorer. The rich are also more extravagant and more fond of displaying their wealth, for, to the great majority of them wealth is a novelty. Shoddy and petroleum, as well as successful speculation, have made millionaires and thrice millionaires of men of low and vulgar minds, destitute of social refinement and gentle breeding, whose wives and daughters know no way of commanding consideration or of attracting admiration, but by their furs and diamonds and their extravagant expenditures. The effect of this on the community at large, in producing a competition in extravagance, and enhancing the average expense and difficulty of living, is not easily estimated. There is no country in the world where the general extravagance is so great as in our own, or where the cost of living is greater for all classes. Some provision is made for paupers as for prisoners and criminals, but there is a larger class who are too honest to steal, too proud to beg, and too high-spirited to allow themselves to be sent to the almshouse; mostly women, many of them widows with one, two, or more children, whose sufferings from want of sufficient food, decent clothing, and comfortable shelter, are not to be told. I attribute the sufferings of these to the delusive doctrine of equality, and the worship of wealth which democracy encourages, and the disgrace it attaches to poverty, and to humble labor for a living; for otherwise most of them could find relief and ample provision for their wants in domestic service. A really hereditary aristocracy produces no such evil, for between them and such aristocracy there is no competition. It is the burgher aristocracy and burgher wealth that treat poverty as a crime or a nuisance, and make our women and girls of American parentage shrink from domestic service as hardly less disgraceful than a life of shame.

The corruption generated by the struggle for wealth which democracy stimulates, is not confined to private and domestic life. It pervades public life. Senor Calderon de la Barca, the Spanish minister for several years to our government at Washington, told me in April, 1852, that when he was first sent by his government to ours at Washington, in 1822, he was charmed with every thing he saw or heard. "The government struck me," he said, "as strictly honest, and your statesmen as remarkable for their public spirit, integrity, and incorruptibility. I was subsequently sent to Mexico; and when recalled from that mission, I was offered my choice between Rome and Washington, such was my high opinion of the American republic, and the honesty and integrity of its government, that I chose Washington in preference to Rome, though the latter was more generally coveted. I have been here now for several years a close observer, and I have seen every thing change under my eyes. All my admiration for the republic and for republican government has vanished. I cannot conceive a government more corrupt than this government of yours. I see men come here worth only their salary as members of congress, and in two or four years return home worth from a hundred thousand to two hundred thousand dollars."—This was said in 1852, when corruption was very little in comparison with what it has become. In 1822, the great body of the people were far from being democratized, and no party in the country bore or would consent to bear the democratic name. There was no democratic party in the country known as such, till after the inauguration of General Jackson as president, March 4, 1829; and none became predominantly democratic, till the success of the democratic Whigs in 1840, who far outdid the Jackson-Van Buren party in their democracy. The late Horace Greeley always called that party the "sham democracy," and treated at first the Whig party, and, after 1856, the Republican party, as the genuine Simon-Pure democracy. He was right in one sense; for the Whig-Republican party was always further gone in democracy, that is, in asserting the supremacy of the popular will and the exclusion of the moral order from politics, than was the party that bore the democratic name.

Up to the election of General Jackson, the American people, if adopting the democratic theory, were not governed by it; they still were influenced by ante-revolutionary traditions, recognized the moral order, the rule of right to which the people as the state as well as individuals were bound to conform; and I believed then and believe now that no purer government, indeed, no better government, existed under heaven. But since then the democratic principle has passed from theory into the practical life of the people, and become the ruling principle of their political judgments and conduct, at least, to an alarming extent. The result we saw during the war, and still more plainly see in the corruption developed by the recent very imperfect investigations in congress. We were told the main facts with regard to the credit mobilier over two years ago; and the real facts are far more damaging than any that appear from the investigation in congress. But this, though perhaps on a larger scale, is yet in reality no grosser than the corruption that has for years obtained in congress, the state legislatures, the municipal governments, and the elections all over the country. It is in vain to look to legislation for a remedy. The laws are good enough as they are, and stringent enough; but laws are impotent where the people have become venal, and are easily evaded or openly violated with impunity, when they are not consecrated and rendered inviolable by the national conscience: and it is of the essence of democracy to dispense with conscience, and to attempt to maintain wise and beneficent government, without drawing on the moral order, by considerations of public and private utility alone.

The actual burden imposed by our democratic administrations, whether called Democratic or Republican, and including both the general government and the several state governments, due to the democratic principle itself, cannot be even approximately ascertained. The extravagance of the American people, and the expensiveness of their style of living in proportion to their means, we attribute to democracy, which measures a man's respectability by his wealth, and his wealth by his expenditures; for the American people are naturally both frugal and economical. The American people are directly and indirectly more heavily taxed by government, counting the general government and the state and municipal governments, than any other people known. The population of the United States, and that of France before her late dismemberment, are about equal; and yet the taxes imposed by our government are more than double the taxes imposed by the French government; and if we have to provide for the expenses of a disastrous civil war, France has to provide for the expenses and losses of an equally disastrous foreign war, carried on in her own territory. The cost of living in this country should be much less than in any European country, owing to the average mildness of our climate, the extent, fertility, and cheapness of land, and the variety of its productions; and yet the cost of living with us, I am told, is greater even than in England, the dearest country in Europe, and which is obliged to import annually from a hundred million to a hundred and fifty million dollars' worth of breadstuffs and provisions to feed her population. We attribute this to democracy, as we do the dearness of living in England; for England is almost as democratic as the United States. The election of a president once every four years costs the American people, besides the derangement of business, more than the civil list of Great Britain costs the British people. The aristocracy is hardly a check on the commons; and as not engaged in business, and living on its own revenues derived principally from land and mines, hardly affects the course of the business operations of the nation, or the general cost and style of living. In

Italy and Germany the democratic principle, combined with the monarchical form, prevails; and in both taxation is rapidly approaching the British and the American standard, notwithstanding the confiscation of the goods of the church by the former, and the heavy French indemnity to the latter.

But we have singularly failed to make ourselves understood, if the reader infers that we are defending monarchy or aristocracy, or that we have had any other purpose in our remarks than to show that the assertion of the people as the source of all legitimate authority, and that governments derive all their just powers from the assent of the governed, which makes all authority, all law of purely human origin, excludes the divine order which alone has authority for conscience, divorces politics from ethics, substitutes utility for right, and makes it the measure of justice, fails of the end of all just government, the promotion of the public good, and is either no government at all, but a mere agency of the controlling private interests of the people, or a government of mere force. This with me is no new doctrine: I defended it in the *Democratic Review* thirty years ago, while I was yet a Protestant, and it has been steadily maintained in this *Review* from its first number in January, 1844. To assert and defend it, was a main purpose for which I originally commenced it.

Now, it is easy to see that what we object to is not popular government, but the doctrine that the people as the state or nation are the origin and source of all authority and all law, that they are absolutely supreme, and bound by no law or authority that does not emanate from themselves. We call this the democratic principle; but as the people are here taken in the sense of state or nation, it may be applied equally to any political order which asserts the national will as supreme and free from all authority or law which does not emanate from the nation itself. The principle is applied in Russia, where the czar, as representing the nation, claims absolute autocratic power; it is applied in Germany in a more absolute sense than in the United States, and is the principle on which Prince von Bismarck suppresses the Jesuits and kindred religious orders, and expels them from the empire, and on which he persecutes the church, denies her independence, and demands the enactment of statutes that subject her to the imperial will, that is, the national authority. It is the principle on which the London *Times* asserted the other day that no Catholic can be a loyal Englishman, and on which the sectarian press of this country maintain that we cannot be Catholics and loyal American citizens. It is the principle which inspires and underlies the whole revolutionary party in Europe. It is the liberty of the people, not from aristocracies, kings, kaisers, or arbitrary power, but from all authority or law, that does not emanate from the people, or from the nation, and therefore from a purely human source, that the party is struggling for. That is, the revolutionary party, and democratic party of Europe, are struggling to eliminate from modern society the *jus gentium* of Roman jurisprudence under the protection of religion, or what Lord Arundel of Wardour calls the "law of nations," that is, a law emanating from God himself, and founding and binding the national conscience; and, in this struggle, the mass of the American people sympathize with them, and loudly applaud them.

This is what our age calls liberty, what it means by liberty of conscience, that is, getting rid of all laws that bind the national conscience, and thus severing politics from the moral order, and subjecting the moral order itself to the secular authority, however constituted. The moral order, that is, justice, eternal and immutable right, or the law of nations, is by the divine will and appointment, according to Christian tradition, placed in charge of the pope, or the vicar of Christ on earth. To effect this object and emancipate politics from the law of nations, or the people, the state, or the nation, from the law of eternal and immutable right, that is, the law of God, it is necessary to get rid of the papacy, and to effect the utter destruction of the Catholic Church, its divinely appointed defender; and we see that the democratic, the liberal party, are willing to sustain so unmitigated a despot as the chancellor of the new German empire, if he will only join them in their war against the papacy, and aid them in their efforts to effect the complete destruction of the church. It is to conciliate and gain the support of this liberal party that the several governments of Europe, even of Catholic nations, have abandoned the papacy, even when they have not, like Germany, Italy, and Spain, turned against the pope. No head could wear a crown, no government could stand a day, at least, according to all human calculations, were it to take up the defence of the papacy, or adhere to it, as did the Frank Emperor Charlemagne.

We have called the attention of our readers to the principle that, as we have said, inspires and underlies this so-called liberal party, because it is precisely the principle that in our country is called the democratic principle. As thousands, perhaps, hundreds of thousands of Catholics in the Old World, have been led to adopt and defend this principle, without understanding its real character; so some Catholics in our own country, fired by political ambition, and engrossed in political affairs, may have also been led to adopt it in equal ignorance of its real anticatholic character, supposing they might adopt it and act on it, without injury to the church, or detriment to their Catholic faith and influence. We do not write with any expectation of undeceiving these, if any such there are. If they read us at all, they will not understand us, and will feel towards us only anger and contempt. But there is a large class of Catholic young men, graduates from our colleges, whose minds are fresh and malleable, whose hearts are open and ingenuous, who love truth and justice, and who take a deep interest in the future of their country. We write for them to warn them against the dangers which threaten us, and against which there were none to warn us when we were young like them.

There is also even a larger number of Catholic young women annually coming forth from our conventual schools and academies, with fresh hearts, and cultivated minds, and noble aspirations, who are no less interested in the welfare of the country, and no less capable of exerting an influence on its destiny. They have no more sympathy than we have, with so-called "strong-minded women," who give from the rostrum or platform public lectures on politics or ethics; but we have much mistaken the training they have received from the good sisters who have educated them, if they have not along with the accomplishments that fit them to grace the drawing-room, received that high mental culture which prepares them to be wives and mothers of men; or, if such should be their vocation, to be accomplished and efficient teachers in their turn. Men are but half men, unless inspired and sustained in whatever is good and noble by woman's sympathy and cooperation. We want no *bas bleus,* no female pedants, nor male pedants either, as to that matter; but we do want cultivated, intelligent women, women who not only love their country, but understand its interests and see its dangers, and can, in their proper sphere, exert a domestic and social influence to elevate society and protect it from the principles and corruption which lead to barbarism. This is no time and no country in which to waste one's life in frivolities or on trifles: *Ernst ist das Leben.* And seriously should those of either sex whom the world has not yet corrupted, soured, or discouraged, take it, and labor to perform its high and solemn duties.

What we want, what the church wants, what the country wants, is a high-toned Catholic public opinion, independent of the public opinion of the country at large, and in strict accordance with Catholic tradition and Catholic inspirations, so strong, so decided that every Catholic shall feel it, and yield intelligently and lovingly to its sway. It is to you, my dear Catholic young men and Catholic young women, with warm hearts, and cultivated minds, and noble aims, that I appeal to form and sustain such a true Catholic public opinion. You, with the blessing of God and directed by your venerable pastors, can do it. It is already forming, and you can complete it. Every good deed done, every pure thought breathed, every true word spoken, shall quicken some intelligence, touch some heart, inspire some noble soul. Nothing true or good is ever lost, no brilliant example ever shines in vain. It will kindle some fire, illumine some darkness, and gladden some eyes. Be active, be true, be heroic, and you will be successful beyond what you can hope.

INDEX